Izumi Tsubaki
11
MONTHLY
GIRLS'
NOZAKI

MONTHLY GIRLS' NOZAKI-KUN 11

contents

[ISSUE 99]

NOZAKI'S INTEL

HUH? THERE'S A GIRL IN AN UNFAMILIAR UNIFORM OVER THERE.
WHAT SCHOOL IS THAT FROM?
URO (WANDER)
URO
I'M PRETTY SURE IT'S THE FANCY GIRLS' SCHOOL THREE STATIONS AWAY.
AN ALL-GIRLS SCHOOL...

OH!
SHE LOOKED THIS WAY!!!
SHE'S REALLY CUTE!!!
AHH.
THE GIRLS AT THAT SCHOOL AREN'T USED TO GUYS, SO SHE'S GONNA RUN AWAY.
JUST WATCH.

TA (DASH)
HEY!!!
SHE'S RUNNING STRAIGHT AT US!!!
HUH ...!? THAT'S WEIRD ...
I THOUGHT THE ONLY MEN THEY'D TALK TO ARE, LIKE, TEACHERS ...

UM!
MAY I ASK YOU A QUES-TION...
... SEN-SEI!?
SO IT'S TRUE ...

JUST GOING WITH THE FLOW

HUH !!? YOU'RE NOT A TEACHER !!?
O-OH MY. I'M SO VERY SORRY ...!!!

YOU MUST BE AN ADMINISTRATOR!!
MY APOLOGIES.
UH ... YEAH ...
DON'T JUST ACCEPT IT!

AHH!
AND I EVEN INTERRUPTED WHILE YOU WERE IN THE MIDST OF A CONVERSATION...!!!
YOU WERE JUST SCOLDING THIS PERSON, WEREN'T YOU!?
HUH?
DON'T MIND ME. PLEASE CONTINUE !!!
PLEASE!!!
NO, UH ...
I...!

MIKOSHIBA... YOU HAVE TO WEAR YOUR TIE PROPERLY!
I'M DISAPPOINTED IN YOU.
WHY ARE YOU GOING ALONG WITH IT!!?
JUST FIGHT BACK ALREADY!!!

"ONEE-SAMA"

IN FACT, I CAME IN SEARCH OF MY ONEE-SAMA.
BUT I HAVE BEEN UNABLE TO FIND HER...

ONEE-SAMA ...!?
THERE AREN'T ANY GIRLS WHO LOOK LIKE THEY'RE THIS CUTIE'S BIG SISTER...!!
MAYBE THEY DON'T LOOK ALIKE!?
SISTERS WHO DON'T LOOK ALIKE...
DON'T TELL ME IT'S SOME REALLY COMPLEX FAMILY RELATION-SHIP...

I ATTEMPTED TO SPEAK WITH HER THIS MORNING, BUT SHE SEEMED RATHER BUSY...
SHE'S TOTALLY AVOIDING YOU...!!!
SHOULD WE REALLY GET INVOLVED ...!?
THIS COULD GET PRETTY NASTY...

HER NAME ...
...IS YUU KASHIMA ...
KASHIMA-KUUUN! ♡
KASHIMA-KUUUN! ♡
ONEE-SAMAAA! ♡
SHE'S JUST ANOTHER KASHIMA GROUPIE !!?

HARD TO RESPOND

THEY DECIDED TO BRING HER WITH THEM.
YOU SURE IT'S OKAY FOR US TO LET HER IN THE SCHOOL?
SHE'S NOT GONNA BE SCARED OF THE GUYS, IS SHE?
HMMM.
WELL, THAT SCHOOL ONLY HAS UP TO JUNIOR HIGH, SO I'M A LITTLE WORRIED...
...HOW SHE'LL REACT...
OH MY!!!

UM!!! ARE THE TWO OF THEM DATING!!?
HE'S CARRYING THAT GIRL'S BAG!!!
I'M GONNA GO DROP OFF THE LOG, SO YOU HOLD THIS.
GOT IT.
NO... THEY'RE JUST A COUPLE OF CLASS-MATES...

THEN THE TWO OF THEM MUST BE DATING!!!
IT'S AN AFTER-SCHOOL DATE!!!
THIS FRY BREAD IS REALLY GOOD.
BUT AREN'T THE CURRY BUNS BETTER?
NO... THEY'RE JUST HUNGRY...

OH!
THOSE TWO ARE GAZING DEEPLY AT EACH OTHER!!!
THEY SIMPLY MUST BE DATING!!!
SHE'S KINDA REACTING THE SAME WAY AN UNPOPULAR GUY WOULD...

WE'RE THE ONES WHO SAID IT!?

HEEEY, WAKA! LET'S HANG OUT!
BASHI (SMACK)
BWA-HA-HA-HA-HA!
OH MY!!!

I CANNOT BELIEVE A YOUNG MAN AND WOMAN WOULD BE IN SUCH CLOSE CONTACT...
AHH...
OH, IT'S WAKAMATSU AND SEO ...
HOW SCANDALOUS!!!
THAT'S PROBABLY WHAT SHE'LL SAY...
SERIOUSLY...

I IMAGINE THOSE TWO...
...ARE NOT ONLY DATING ...
...BUT ALSO MUST BE IN A PHYSICAL RELATIONSHIP...

HOW SCANDALOUS !!!

HER DELUSIONAL CAST

HUH? WHATCHA DOING?
ぽん
PON (PAT)
HEY!
WHERE'D YOU COME FROM ...!?
!!!

STOP!!!
DON'T DRAG ME INTO THIS !!!

HUH? WHAT?
YOU PLAYIN' A GAME?
ALL RIGHT! TAAG!!
EEK!
STOP !!!
!!!

HUH ...!?
I'M NOT PART OF IT ...!?

STAY AWAY FROM ME

MISTER ADMINISTRATOR, YOU'RE AN ADULT.
YOU MUSTN'T GO AFTER CHILDREN, YOU KNOW.
THAT MUCH IS COMMON SENSE...
BUT WHY...?
!!!

WHAT'S GOING ON ...!?
NOZAKI-KUN...
...IS WITH A CUTE GIRL ...!!!

HAH!
SAKU-RA!!!
DON'T !!!
STAY AWAY !!!
!!!
NO WAY ...
IS HE TELL-ING ME NOT TO INTRUDE ...!?

YOU'RE GONNA MAKE ME A CRIMINAL ...!!!
WHAT DOES THAT MEAN ...!!?
IT JUST LOOKS BAD...!!!

HER DELUSIONAL CAST ②

SHE'S NOT USED TO COED ENVIRONMENTS BECAUSE SHE'S BEEN AT A GIRLS' SCHOOL SINCE ELEMENTARY SCHOOL...

I-I SEE...

...SO EVERYONE LOOKS LIKE A COUPLE TO HER...

I SEE. I SEE...
PITA (STICK)
SU (SLIDE) SU SU SU
!!
!!!

Look!!!
We're a couple!!! A couple!!!
You can imagine flirting!!!
You can even fantasize about us doing something more extreme!!!
COME ON, COME ON!!!
DOKI (BADUM) DOKI DOKI

THE FLOWER BLOOMED!
I'M SO PROUD...
BUT WHY!!?
HONOBONO (HEARTWARMING)

AS A SHOUJO MANGA-KA

IN ANY CASE, I CANNOT BELIEVE HOW COMMON RELATION-SHIPS ARE IN A COED ENVIRON-MENT.
IT IS EXACTLY AS I READ.
THOSE THREE MUST BE IN A LOVE TRIANGLE ...
WHAT SORT OF BOOKS ARE YOU READING ...?

High school students at coed schools think of nothing but love, from dawn until dusk.
Even tests and sports are all about win-ning over the hand of the girl, you know...
I WISH THAT WERE MY LIFE...
WHAT SORT OF MESSED-UP BOOKS ARE YOU READING?

HMPH!! HOW RUDE! THEY ARE AMAZINGLY INTERESTING SHOUJO MANGA!
SHOUJO MANGA ...?
HAAH...
HON-ESTLY ...
IT FEELS LIKE SHE'S MAKING FUN OF SHOUJO MANGA. THIS IS BAD.
WHAT KIND OF PERSON IS CREATING THIS STUFF ...?

LOOK AT THIS!
④
夢野 咲子
I AM !!!

BOOK: LET'S FALL IN LOVE♡ ④ SAKIKO YUMENO

OKAY. I GET IT

YUMENO-SENSEI'S WORKS ARE SO AMAZING!!!
NOT ONLY IS SUZUKI-KUN COOL...
...BUT I CANNOT HELP BUT IDENTIFY WITH MAMIKO AND HER DELICATE, MAIDENLY HEART.

ぱっ
BA (FWOOSH)
I GET IT. STOP LOOKING AT ME.
YOU'RE REALLY HAPPY.

HOWEVER, IT IS BOTHER-SOME THAT THIS PROMISE, "LET'S GO TO THE AQUARIUM NEXT TIME!♡" HAS NOT BEEN FULFILLED YET.
RIGHT HERE, IN VOLUME ONE.
THIS IS YUMENO-SENSEI, SO I IMAGINE SHE IS USING IT TO FORE-SHADOW SOME MAJOR EVENT IN THE FUTURE...

ぱぱっ
BABA
I GET IT. JUST STOP LOOKING AT ME!
YOU TOTALLY FORGOT ABOUT THAT.

AN ACCEPTING AND SINCERE GIRL

HE CAME CLEAN.

WHAA—!!?

YOU ARE SAKIKO YUMENO-SENSEI!!?

I-I LOVE READING YOUR WORK...!!!
SHE BE-LIEVED HIM...!!!
SHE BE-LIEVED HIM RIGHT AWAY...!!!
SO ACCEPTING...!!!

UM...!
MAY I SHAKE YOUR HAND...!!?
OH, BUT OUR TEACHERS FORBADE US FROM...
...TOUCHING MEN'S HANDS WITHOUT A GOOD REASON...

BUT IF I WRAP YOUR HAND IN THIS TOWEL...
THEN WE SHAN'T TOUCH...
GYU (WRAP)
GYU
SO SIN-CERE...!!!
BUT IT'S LIKE SHE'S TOUCHING SOME-THING DIRTY. THAT'S KINDA RUDE.
RIGHT?

SHE SAID IT AT THE START

YOU SURE ABOUT THIS?
JUST TELLING HER LIKE THAT...?
ISN'T THAT DANGEROUS TO DO WITH A FAN?
WELL...
...IT'S NOT LIKE I'M GONNA SEE HER AGAIN.
AND KASHIMA WON'T GOSSIP WITH ME ABOUT ONE OF HER FANS.

OKAY, I'LL SIGN THIS FOR YOU.
SINCE YOU HAVE THE BOOK WITH YOU.
DO YOU REALLY MEAN IT!?
YEAH.
SO, UH, YOUR NAME IS...?

IT'S REI...
...KA-SHIMA!

THE LITTLE SISTER!!?
?
NOZAKI'S PERSONAL INFO WAS LATER LEAKED, BY WAY OF KASHIMA.

OHH?
YOU'RE NOT VERY TALL, ARE YOU?
SO YOU'RE KASHIMA'S SISTER?
GUI (TUG)
GUI
AHH!
THAT COUPLE FROM EARLIER ...!!!
HUH?
WE'RE CLEARLY JUST A SENPAI AND HER KOUHAI!
HERE— LOOK HARDER!
GUI
GUI
I—
I AM SO SORRY...!!! I MUST HAVE BEEN MIS-TAKEN...
HEH HEH HEH...
MAKES SENSE FOR A JUNIOR HIGH KID...
...TO BE SCARED OF SEO ...
I GET IT.
IN OTHER WORDS ...
... YOU'RE A SENPAI WHO FORCED HER KOUHAI ...
...INTO A PHYSICAL RELA-TION-SHIP!!
YOU'RE REALLY SOME-THING ELSE ...!!!
YOU MUST HAVE SOME QUITE EXTREME TASTES!!!

[ISSUE 100]

THE KASHIMA SISTERS

SHE FOUND HER SISTER.
HUH!?
WHAT'RE YOU DOING HERE, REI...!!?

YOU FORGOT TO BRING YOUR HOUSE KEY WITH YOU.
YOU'RE SO FORGETFUL.
UMM...
I REALLY SHOULD'VE CHECKED TO MAKE SURE I HAD IT THIS MORNING.
I WAS PRETTY BUSY, THOUGH.
THEY REALLY ARE SISTERS...
THEY STILL DON'T LOOK ALIKE...

SO NOZAKI'S AN ADMINISTRATOR, HMMM...?
NIYA (GRIN)
NIYA
OHHH?
I SEE.
THE OLDER SISTER'S PRETTY RUDE...

ONEE-SAMA!!! IT IS SIMPLY NOT DONE TO CALL YOUR ELDERS BY NAME LIKE THAT!!!
ESPECIALLY SOMEONE WHO IS AT LEAST EIGHT YEARS OLDER THAN YOU!!
HONESTLY!
THE YOUNGER ONE'S PLENTY RUDE TOO...

BUT THEY ARE IMPORTANT

HUH!!? YOU'RE A STUDENT !?
UHH ... WELL ... ...
YEAH.
HAH!
OH YES!!! IN THE MAGAZINE, I DO BELIEVE I SAW IT...

IT REALLY IS WRITTEN RIGHT HERE!!!
FRESH ONE-SHOT
al-life high school girl Sakiko Yumeno
YOU'RE A HIGH SCHOOL GIRL, AREN'T YOU!!?
YUMENO-SENSEI!!!!

DO YOU HONESTLY BELIEVE THAT WHEN NOZAKI IS STANDING RIGHT THERE ...!!?
FIRST OF ALL, THAT SELF-PORTRAIT HAS HUGE RINGLETS ...!!!
COME ON, NOZAKI!!! JUST SAY IT!!!

SU (FWISH)
THAT'S RIGHT.
HE'S WAY TOO WEAK WHEN DEALING WITH FANS!!!

MY CUTE LITTLE SISTER

HUH? COME TO THINK OF IT, WHERE'S KASHIMA-KUN?
HER SISTER WANTED TO WATCH REHEARSAL, SO SHE WENT TO GO TALK TO THEM ABOUT IT.
THE DRAMA CLUB.
HEE HEE.
SHE REALLY CARES ABOUT HER SISTER.
RIGHT?

HEY, EVERY-ONE!!!
MY LITTLE SISTER CAME TO VISIT, SO IS IT OKAY IF SHE SITS IN ON REHEARS-AL!?

HUH?
YOUR LITTLE SISTER !?
I WANNA SEE HER!
SURE THING!
GO GET HER!!
REALLY !?
THEN ...

...GUYS, STEP AWAY FROM THE GIRLS.
EITHER THAT, OR HIDE YOUR IDENTITY BY CROSS-DRESSING.
AND MAKE IT BELIEVABLE...
WHAT'S COMING ...!!?

A LADY IS COMING!!!

OHHH, SHE GOES TO AN ALL-GIRLS SCHOOL, SO SHE'S NOT USED TO GUYS!
I-GET-IT.
WHAT SORT OF THINGS HAPPEN WHEN GUYS AND GIRLS ARE TO-GETH-ER?
DOES SHE GO, "GET AWAY FROM EACH OTHER AT ONCE!!"?
WELL ...

SHE GETS SOME PRETTY INDECENT THOUGHTS.
I-INDE-CENT ...!!?

SHE MAKES UP FOR NOT KNOWING ABOUT THE REAL WORLD WITH AN OVERACTIVE IMAGINA-TION...
JUST SEEING A GUY AND GIRL TOGETHER MAKES HER TREAT THEM LIKE A COUPLE...
OHH!!
THAT KINDA THING!!
I DON'T THINK A PROPER LITTLE LADY'S IMAGINA-TION IS SOMETHING TO WORRY ABOUT!!
YOU SAY COUPLE, BUT I BET IT'S JUST THEM HOLDING HANDS!
AH-HA-HA-HA-HA-HA-HA-HA!

THEY'RE ALL PRETTY MUCH NAKED.
WITH JUST FLOWERS.
A WEIRDO IS COMING!!!

THE KASHIMA BLOODLINE

I apologize for intruding on such short notice.

My name is Rei Kashima.

WHOOOOOA!!
SHE'S CUTE!!!
SHE'S REALLY CUTE!!!
THE KASHIMA BLOODLINE RUNS TRUE, HORI-CHAN!!!
DON'T LOOK AT ME.

OKAY, REI.
YOU SIT HERE.
SU (FWISH)
... YES ... ONEE-SAMA.
SUSU
WHOOOOOA!
EVERY MOVE SHE MAKES IS GORGEOUS!!!
SHE'S TOTALLY KASHIMA-KUN'S SISTER!!!
WOW!!!

LISTEN UP.
YOU HAVE TO STAY RIGHT HERE. NO GETTING UP AND WALKING AROUND ON A WHIM.
WE CAN'T HAVE YOU WANDERING AROUND.
GOT IT?
SHE REALLY IS KASHIMA-KUN'S SISTER...

REI-SAMA'S GREAT DEDUCTION

OH YES. PERHAPS AT THE DRAMA CLUB...

KYORO (GLANCE) きょろ…

...I MIGHT FIND A BOY ONEE-SAMA IS INTERESTED IN...

WAI (CHATTER) わい
WAI わい
WAI わい
JI (STARE) じっ…

GO STAND OVER THERE.
OKAY!
!
I KNOW!!

IT MUST BE THIS PERSON ...!!!
CHIRA (PEEK) ちらっ
WHY ME!!?
I DIDN'T SAY ANYTHING!!!

WE ALL KNOW

AFTER ALL, ONEE-SAMA ...
...IS LIKE A COOL, BEAUTIFUL YOUNG MAN...
IN WHICH CASE, HER PARTNER ...

...MUST BE A PRETTY BOY WHO IS HER EXACT OPPOSITE. ♡
I— I'M A GUY !!!
I'LL ... ... PROTECT YOU!!
HE'S SMALL ... ...BUT HE'S STILL A GUY...

OR THEY BOTH NEED TO BE VERY AWARE OF EACH OTHER.
WE'RE BOTH THE SAME HEIGHT AGAIN.
YOU CAN LEAN ON ME JUST FOR NOW.
DAM-MIT ...!!!
GUSU (SNIFFLE)
ぐすっ
I'M GONNA GET TALLER THAN YOU. JUST WAIT!!
THEY NEED TO BE RIVALS ...!!

I TO-TALLY GET IT!!!
YOU HAVE THE BEST TASTE !!!
WHA...? I KINDA FEEL LIKE I'M ON THE AWAY TEAM...

WISE COUNSEL

OH!! BUT LOOK AT THAT, YUMENO-SENSEI!!!
THE RE-HEARSAL HAS BEGUN!!
THOSE TWO ARE PLAYING LOVERS.
HOW WON-DER-FUL!!

STILL, I DO BE-LIEVE THAT BOY...
...HAS FEELINGS FOR THE GIRL SITTING IN THE BACK.
FOR SOME TIME, HE HAS BEEN GLANCING IN HER DIRECTION!
I SEE.
IN ADDITION, THAT IS THE FACE OF SOME-ONE WHO WANTS TO SEE HOW SHE REACTS...
...TO WATCH-ING HIS LOVE SCENE.
IT'S GOT TO BE!

Then, under all that pressure, she finally makes her move!!
SHE SNEAKS INTO HIS BEDROOM, DOES SHE NOT!?
Yeah, she sneaks into his bed-room ...
IN A SLINKY NEGLI-GEE ...!!!

...IS THIS EROTICA ...?
IT'S A BIT, YOU KNOW...
HOW ...?

PAY ATTENTION TO ME

WHAT DO I DO...? THEY'RE GETTING REALLY INTO IT...
I...
I SHOULD JOIN IN TOO ...!!!

UMM, THOSE TWO LOOK PRETTY CLOSE, DON'T THEY!?
REALLY CLOSE!!
NOT THOSE TWO.
LOVE WILL NEVER BLOOM BETWEEN THOSE TWO.
THEY'LL ALWAYS PREFER BEING JUST FRIENDS.

OH!
THOSE TWO LOOK LIKE THEY DON'T GET ALONG!! BUT I BET THEY'LL FIND COMMON GROUND SOON!!
SOMETHING LIKE, "IT WAS A TOTAL MISUNDERSTANDING!"
THEY'LL NEVER GET ALONG.
THEY'RE SUPER-INCOMPATIBLE.
THEIR NATURES WILL ALWAYS CLASH...
BUT INDEED, THAT HAS ITS OWN APPEAL.
THE AESTHETICS OF PARALLEL LINES.

ぴーっ
PIII (SOB)
ORO (PANIC)
オロ
ORO
オロ
ORO
オロ
ORO
オロ
LOOKS LIKE HER WIN...

PLEASE, SAKURA-SENPAI

OH YES.
THERE IS SOMETHING I WOULD LIKE TO ASK YOU, SAKURA-SENPAI...
YOU THINK I'LL BE ABLE TO GIVE YOU AN ANSWER...?
ぐすっ
GUSU (SNIFFLE)
PLEASE—COULD YOU TELL ME WHICH OF THESE BOYS...
...ONEE-SAMA IS CLOSE TO!?

THAT'S GOT TO BE THE PRESIDENT, HORI-SENPAI.
IS THAT IT?
......
HOW ODD...
HE IS RATHER SHORT, YOU CAN HARDLY CALL HIM A PRETTY BOY...
HE SEEMS FAIRLY STRAITLACED TOO...

NO...!!! EVEN SO, THIS IS THE DRAMA CLUB!! PERHAPS...!!!
SA-KURA-SAMA!!
MIGHT I ASK ONE MORE FAVOR...!!?

UM... SENPAI...
"ARE YOU GOOD AT CROSS-DRESS-ING?"
...SHE ASKS.
INTER-PRETING
HURH!!?
ギッ
GI (GLARE)

MY PRECIOUS ONEE-SAMA

YES... IF HE SHOULD HAPPEN TO BE A SKILLED CROSS-DRESSER ...
A BEAUTY IN MEN'S CLOTHING
A LOVELY YOUNG MAN
...THERE WOULD BE NOTHING TO PREVENT ME FROM ACCEPTING HIM AS HER PARTNER ...!!!

I SUPPOSE I WILL BE SLIGHTLY LONELY IF I LOSE MY PRECIOUS ONEE-SAMA, BUT...
WHAAA—?
SO YOU REALLY DO WANT TO WEAR GIRLS' CLOTHES AFTER A—?
OOF!
BESHI (SMACK)

DO (THUD)
......
...OH.
WHOOPS.
......
......
......

...SO...
...DOES WOMEN'S CLOTHING SUIT YOU?
YOU SURE YOU SHOULD JUST IGNORE THAT!!?
YOU KNOW, YOUR SISTER'S ON THE FLOOR!!!

PLENTY TO WORRY ABOUT

OH!!!
MORE IMPORTANTLY, I SEE A COUPLE IN THE SHADOWS...!!!
THAT'S JUST THE WINGS!!!
TA (TMP) たたた TA TA
......
SORRY FOR DOING THAT IN FRONT OF YOUR SISTER ...
YOU'VE GOT YOUR DIGNITY AS THE OLDER SIBLING TO WORRY ABOUT...
NO, IT'S OKAY.

I'M PRETTY SURE IT WOULD'VE BEEN WORSE FOR US IF YOU HAD PET MY HEAD OR SOME-THING...
SHE WOULD'VE STRIPPED US NAKED ...
WHAT IS WITH YOUR SISTER ...?

BUT Y'KNOW, I NEVER THOUGHT SHE'D GET FRIENDLY WITH NOZAKI...
HE'S SO BIG...
SPEAKING OF NOZAKI, WHAT'S WITH THE WEIRD HAIR...?
WHAT EVEN IS THAT?
HUH? OH, YOU'RE RIGHT...
THAT HAIR-STYLE...

MAYBE ...
...SHE THINKS HE'S A GIRL...
A GIRL WITH PIGTAILS ...
WHAT IS WITH YOUR SISTER ...!?

THE PROBLEMS THEY LEFT BEHIND

IN THE END, BOTH SISTERS CAUSED A BUNCH OF PROBLEMS BEFORE THEY LEFT...
I'M BEAT...
HOW'D YOU GET HERE IN THE FIRST PLACE?
I TOOK A TAXI!
YEAH... WELL, SHE'S A GOOD GIRL.
WEAK TO HIS FANS

BUT WHAT'S SAKURA DOING?
?
ブツ
BUTSU (MUTTER)
ARROGANT GUYS...
CHILDHOOD FRIENDS...
FIGHTING LIKE CATS AND DOGS...
ブツ
BUTSU
AGE GAP...
SHE SAID SHE HASN'T READ ENOUGH SHOUJO MANGA, SO SHE NEEDS TO STUDY UP.

YOU DON'T NEED TO PUSH YOURSELF, SAKURA!
DON'T TRY TO STOP ME, NOZAKI-KUN!!! I WANT SOMEONE TO TELL ME "I TOTALLY GET IT!!!"
......
パカッ
PAKA (OPEN)
....
演劇部
化粧品

BOX: DRAMA CLUB MAKEUP

NO WAY...
NO FREAKIN' WAY ...!!!
BATAN (SHUT)
バタン

SAKURA-SENPAI'S APPEAL

LOVE WILL NEVER BLOOM BETWEEN THOSE TWO.
THEY'LL ALWAYS PREFER BEING JUST FRIENDS.
THAT...
...IS WHAT I SAID EARLIER...
YEAH.
I MAY HAVE GOTTEN SLIGHTLY CARRIED AWAY SINCE I ARRIVED HERE!!!
BUT EVERYWHERE I LOOK, THERE ARE YOUNG MEN AND WOMEN!!
THERE IS ALWAYS A CHANCE THAT FRIENDSHIP WILL SLIP OVER THE LINE AND BECOME SOMETHING MORE!!!
THAT'S RIGHT!!!
RIGHT... ...NOZAKI-KUN!!?
GUI (TUG)
GUI
HAH!
SAKURA-SAMA...!!!
IF YOU WOULD LIKE SOME CANDY, I HAPPEN TO HAVE SOME WITH ME.
IF IT PLEASES YOU.
I WASN'T BEGGING FOR CANDY!!!

[Extra] HAPPY SISTERS

HORI-SENPAI GOT ALL FLUSTERED LOOKING AT MY CUTE LITTLE SISTER...
HE MUST ...
... ACTUALLY PREFER HER...!!!
WAH!

THAT'S KINDA WHAT I WAS HOPING WOULD HAPPEN.
ME TOO.
HUH ?
SORRY! WE CAN STILL DO IT NOW. LET'S TRY!
JUST WAIT.

SENPAI ...!!
BE-TWEEN ME AND REI...
... WHO'S CUTER !!?
YOUR SISTER.
AND WHO'S COOLER !!?
YOU.
THANKS !!!

GOING HOME.
THOSE TWO ...
... COMPETE ... IN COM-PLETELY DIFFERENT FIELDS...
IT'S NOT EVEN A COMPETITION...

[ISSUE 101]
DEADLINES
DEADLINES
WAIT FOR
NO ONE
WAIT
NO

BETA BLUES

SATURDAY AFTERNOON
SORRY.
I MESSED UP ON MY TIME MANAGEMENT.
WE'RE GONNA BE WORKING RIGHT UP UNTIL THE DEADLINE.

SO, MIKOSHIBA, TAKE CARE OF THE FLOWERS AND DECORATIONS!
AND, WAKAMATSU, APPLY ALL OF THE TONE!!!
OKAY!!!
IS THE BETA ALL DONE?

THE BETA WAS DONE YESTERDAY...
SHE DIDN'T SEEM ALL THAT UP FOR IT...
BY SAKURA.
OH, THERE LOOKS LIKE A LOT THIS TIME!
THIS COULD BE BAD!!!
IT MIGHT TAKE ALL NIGHT!!!
I MIGHT NEED TO STAY OVER!!!
SAKURA, THAT'S WAY TOO OBVIOUS...!!!

BUT...
...ONCE SHE GOT STARTED, IT WENT BY PRETTY QUICKLY. THAT'S A RELIEF.
THIS IS...
...THE LAST PAGE...!
UGH...
YOU FORGOT PARTWAY THROUGH, DIDN'T YOU, SAKURA!!?

OKAY, SENPAI!

MID-NIGHT
WE'VE BEEN WORKING SINCE THE AFTER-NOON.
UTSURO (DAZED)
THIS IS REALLY TIRING...
WHAT PART OF THE FLOWER AM I EVEN DRAWING...?
SEN-PAI... ...ARE YOU OKAY?

WAKA-MATSU, YOU LOOK LIKE YOU'RE DOING JUST FINE...
I GUESS YOU ARE AN ATHLETE, AFTER ALL.
YEAH!!!
I'M REALLY GOOD AT SITTING IN ONE SPOT AND DOING WORK LIKE THIS!!!
WHY DO YOU EVEN PLAY BASKET-BALL?

OKAY, SINCE YOU'RE FEELING SO GREAT, YOU SHOULD DO SOMETHING TO KEEP ME AMPED-UP TOO.
THAT'S AN ORDER FROM YOUR SENPAI!
HUH!? SOME-THING TO AMP YOU UP!!?
UHHHH, UMMM...

UNNECESSARY WORK ①

WHY BUNNY EARS!!?
HUH!?
BUT I THOUGHT YOU LIKED THIS SORT OF THING...!!!
SEEING A BUNNY DUDE ISN'T GONNA GET ME AMPED-UP!!!
BUNNY GIRL
SCREW THAT!!
THE SKIMPY BITS JUST PISS ME OFF EVEN MORE!!!

I'LL GIVE YOU THIS ROUGH SKETCH OF MAMIKO, THEN.
HALF NAKED
IT'S THE APPEAL OF SOMEONE BEFORE THEY GET DRESSED.
AWWW...
BUT EVEN NAKED, MAMIKO'S STILL...
COME ON, DON'T SAY THAT.

ONLY I'VE SEEN MAMIKO WITH THIS SORT OF APPEAL BEFORE, BUT I'LL LET YOU HAVE A BIT OF IT TOO...
......
HMM...? IS THIS REALLY APPEALING...?
NAH... BUT IF I DO THIS HERE... YEAH...
YEAH...

HERE... NOW THIS IS APPEALING, RIGHT?
HI! ♡
YOU REALLY ADDED A LOT, DIDN'T YOU?
SHE'S REALLY FLIRTY.

UNNECESSARY WORK ②

... SPEAKING OF WHICH ...
SHAKA (SKRITCH)
I ALWAYS SEE HER IN HER SCHOOL UNIFORM ...
...SO THIS IS KINDA THROWING ME OFF...
SHAKA
SUTOOON (TA-DAA)

GOOD MORNING... ...EVERYONE!

I'VE GOT BIG NEWS, MAMIKO!!

WE JUST ...
...DON'T LIKE YOU...!!
SORRY. I KNOW YOU'RE TRYING TO BE NICE, BUT JUST STOP, MIKOSHIBA.
I DON'T NEED FLOWERS THERE.

BENEATH THE CALM EXTERIOR

3:00 A.M.
I'M NOT TIRED ANYMORE, BUT I'M KINDA FED UP WITH THIS...
YEAH, I KNOW.
MY FOCUS...
I THINK I'M STARTING TO LOSE IT...

THEN HOW ABOUT I MAKE US A SNACK?
SUKU (STAND)
HUH? UH, THANKS...
...NO-ZAKI!
SORRY TO MAKE YOU STOP WORKING, SENPAI.
ESPECIALLY WHEN YOU WERE CONCEN-TRATING.

Minimum 2 HOURS To Make
SPECIAL ♥ DINNERS

HEY... HE'S THE MOST FED UP WITH IT...!!!
WE HAVE TO STOP HIM...!!!
HE'S GONNA BE COOKING FOR TWO HOURS!
WE HAVE TO STOP HIM...!!!

A POWERFUL HELPER

YOU KNOW HOW SOMETIMES YOU WANT A CHANGE OF SCENERY WHEN YOU'RE STUDYING FOR A TEST?
THIS IS THAT.
PULL YOURSELF TO-GETHER!!!
THIS ISN'T LIKE STUDY-ING FOR A TEST!!!
THIS IS WORSE!!

CALM DOWN. I BROUGHT MAYU HERE FOR SOME-THING LIKE THIS.
スパーン
SUPAAAN (FWOOSH)
MAYU-KUN!!?
HE'S BEEN IN THERE!!?
SINCE WHEN!?

WAIT— SO HE'S OUR PINCH HITTER!!?
IS HE A REALLY GOOD ARTIST OR SOME-THING!?
BUT YOU KNOW, HE DOES KINDA FEEL LIKE SOME SORT OF ULTIMATE WEAPON ...!!!
OKAY, MAYU.

YOU TAKE THAT END.
ガタッ
GATA (CLATTER)
HE'S HERE TO CHANGE THE SCENERY!!?

WHEN IT NEVER ENDS...

Y'KNOW, IT'S WEIRD TO SEE YOU LIKE THIS, NOZAKI.
WELL, I'VE BEEN WORKING FOR THREE DAYS STRAIGHT, SO IT'S JUST A LITTLE MUCH...
I'M SICK OF IT.
GUESS THAT'D MAKE IT HARD FOR ANYTHING TO SEEM FRESH...

I KNOW! IT FEELS FASTER IF YOU TEACH IT TO SOMEONE ELSE.
WHY DON'T YOU TEACH MAYU-KUN HOW TO DO IT WHILE YOU KEEP WORKING?
WHAA...?
THERE'S NO WAY HE'D EVER PLAY ALONG WITH THAT...

...NO.
IF YOU'RE OKAY WITH ME...
...I'LL DO IT.
WHAT...!!?
YOU MEAN... HE'S WILLING TO IGNORE HOW MUCH OF A HASSLE IT IS TO HELP OUT HIS BROTHER...!!?
WHAT A GOOD BROTHER...!!!

I'VE BEEN SLEEPING SINCE LAST NIGHT, SO I'M TIRED OF SLEEPING...
I CAN'T SLEEP ANYMORE.
DAMN YOU, MAYU!!!

HIS BROTHER'S WARM GAZE

OKAY, SO I'LL SHOW YOU HOW I INK.
I USE A G PEN AND A MAPPING PEN.
G PEN
CAN DRAW STRONG LINES WITH VARIABLE WIDTHS
MAPPING PEN
EASILY DRAWS THIN LINES

I USE THE G PEN TO DRAW THE THICK LINES HERE ON THE EDGES.
SHA (SKRITCH)
THAT'S REALLY COOL, NII-SAN.
REALLY ...!!?
!!
WELL, ONCE YOU GET USED TO DOING IT, YOU CAN EVEN DO FINE LINES LIKE THESE ONES!!

WAY TO GO, NII-SAN.
WOW ...!!!
I FEEL A SORT OF ADMIRING LOOK I'VE NEVER GOTTEN FROM HIM BEFORE ...!!!
SHAKA (SCRATCH)
SHAKA
SHAKA
LOOK AT ME MORE!!! LOOK AT YOUR BIG BROTHER!!!
TAKE A GOOD, LONG LOOK AT YOUR BIG BROTHER WHILE HE WORKS!!!

SHAKA
SHAKA
SHAKA
Way to go, Nii-san.
You're really good Nii-san.
YOU'RE REALLY GOOD, NII-SAN.

AN UNEXPECTED REACTION

HE'S BACK, SENPAI!!
SHAKI (SKRITCH)
SHAKI
SHAKI
HE'S PRETTY SIMPLE, AFTER ALL...
ANYWAY, I THINK I'LL WORK ON SOME TONE.
I'M DONE WITH THE FLOWERS.

MIKOTO-SAN.
YOU CAN DO OTHER THINGS THAN DRAW FLOWERS?
That's really cool, Nii-san.
HA HA HA!
YOU'RE NOT GONNA GET ME ALL RILED UP WITH THAT ACT, YOU KNOW!
I'M NOT LIKE NOZAKI!!!!

WAY TO GO, MIKOTO-SAN.
YOU KNOW, THAT REALLY IS COOL!
IT'S NOT JUST FLOWERS BUT TONE TOO!
HA HA HA!
I SAID IT'S NOT GONNA WORK...
YOU HOLDING A BLADE SUITS YOU, MIKOTO-SAN.

HUH...?
R—REALLY...?
SOWA (QUIVER)
I FALTERED...!!!

DO AS SENPAI SAYS

All right! Just sit back, shut up, and watch Mikoshiba-senpai's ...
... glorious blade work, my kouhai!!
KYAA!

SHAAAA (FWIIISH)
SHAKI
SHAKI
......
JI (STARE)
......
JI

JAAAN (TA-DAAA)
WELL...!? ISN'T IT GORGEOUS !?
KICCHIRI (PERFECT)
THAT'S AMAZING, SENPAI!!!
WHOOOA!
WAY TO GO, MIKOTO-SAN.

BUT NAKATANI-KUN'S HAIR IS SUPPOSED TO BE TONE NUMBER SIXTY-FOUR.
THIS ONE!!!
SE-64
DON'T STAY QUIET ABOUT THAT!!!

THE IDIOT JOCK

I KNOW! YOU'RE STRONG, SO YOU CAN PRESS THE TONE!!
PRESS...
...THE TONE...?
?
YOU LAY DOWN A SHEET OF PAPER AND RUB IT AFTER APPLYING TO MAKE SURE IT DOESN'T COME OFF.
GOSHI (RUB)
GOSHI

IT'S EASIEST TO USE ONE OF THE BACKING SHEETS ONCE ALL THE TONE IS GONE FROM IT.
BECAUSE THEY'RE SMOOTH.
ALMOST GONE
TAKE IT ALL OFF
IT'S PRETTY TIRING, SO IT SHOULD HELP WITH STRENGH TRAINING, YOU KNOW.
I SEE...

......
YEAH, YEAH. LIKE THAT!
YOU'RE DOING GREAT.
GOSHI
MOZO (FIDGET)
MOZO
AH HA HA!
TOUGH DOING IT SITTING DOWN, HUH!?
WELL...
HE IS AN ATHLETE, AFTER ALL...

NO... HE'S...
...PUTTING DOWN A LOAD...!!!
HE'S DOING A SQUAT!!

THE ELF DID HIS BEST

5:00 A.M.
ふわああ
FUWAAA (YAAAWN)
I GOTTA GET SOME SLEEP.
I'LL KEEP GOING WHEN I GET UP.
GOOD NIGHT, SENPAI.
OH. THANKS, YOU TWO.

8:00 A.M.
ゴッ
GO (THUD)
...... I SOMEHOW... MANAGED ...
...TO FINISH ... ...INKING...
JUST THE TONE NOW...

......

2:00 P.M.
HUH!? IT'S ALL DONE!!?
YOU COULD'VE WOKEN US UP, NOZAKI-SENPAI...!!!
HEY, WHAT'S WRONG, MAYU?
HUH!?
YOUR LEGS HURT!?
WHAT THE HELL WERE YOU DOING!?

THE ELF'S FOOD

IT'S ... STILL, WHO DID THIS?
IT MUST HAVE BEEN ELVES!!!
WHEN YOU PUT MILK BY THE WINDOWSILL, THE ELVES COME HELP YOU!!
WHAA...?
AN ELF WHO FINISHED PUTTING ON TONE ...?
MIKO-SHIBA-SENPAI ...
... WHAT ARE YOU DOING ...?
...?
WELL... I FIGURED SAKURA MIGHT BE HIDING SOME-WHERE...
BUT SHE'S NOT HERE.
AH HA HA.
I'M PRETTY SURE WE'D REALIZE IF SHE WAS HERE!
REALLY!
HA HA HA ...
......
SENPAI, ISN'T THAT NOZAKI-SENPAI'S UNDER-WEAR...!!?

[ISSUE 102]

SMILE WITH SPARKLY EYES

I THINK ...
...IT'S ABOUT TIME FOR ME TO TELL WAKA, "I'M LORELAI!"...

WHA ...!!?
WELL...
I ALMOST SAID IT BY ACCIDENT THE OTHER DAY.
SO I FIGURE I SHOULD JUST TELL HIM AND GET EVERYTHING OUT IN THE OPEN.
I'VE ALREADY HAD A BUNCH OF FUN WITH IT.

WAIT, WAIT, WAIT !!!
DO YOU HAVE ANY IDEA WHAT HE'LL DO IF YOU JUST TELL HIM THAT...?
WELL ...
I GUESS HE'LL BE PRETTY CONFUSED AT FIRST ...
HUH...? SENPAI'S LORELAI-SAN...?
LORELAI-SAN'S SENPAI...?

BUT THE NEXT DAY, HE'LL HAVE ACCEPTED REALITY!
Lorelai-san is Seo-senpai!!
That makes you twice as amazing a senpai. I love you!!!
DOESN'T IT FEEL LIKE THAT WAKA-MATSU IS COM-PLETELY HIDING FROM REALITY?

A WONDERFUL WAY TO CONFESS

BUT YOU KNOW, I THINK IT'S WAY BETTER TO COME CLEAN NOW THAN WHEN THEY FIRST MET!
THEY'RE GETTING ALONG BETTER NOW!
SA-KURA!?
YEAH, YOU'RE RIGHT!
YEAH, YEAH.

I'M NORMALLY THE TYPE TO GET ALL THE SMALL STUFF OUT IN THE OPEN RIGHT AWAY.
I'M A HUGE FAN OF LORELAI-SAN!!
BWA-HA-HA-HA!
THAT'S ME!!!
OOOOH!
THEN HOW DO YOU PLAN ON TELLING HIM?

HMM ...? UH, WELL ...
I'LL CALL HIM OUT TO THE REAR GARDEN ...
THE REAR GAR-DEN!!!
THAT'S GREAT!!
I'LL BE HIDING IN THE BUSHES ...
OHHH!!
SO GOOD !!
AND THEN ...?
わく
WAKU (EXCITED)
わく
WAKU

WELL, IT'LL BE LIKE THIS.
ざばぁっ
ZABAA (FWOOOSH)
I'm Lorelai!!
テッテレ!!
TETTEREE (OUTDUDULU)
THAT'S REALLY CRUDE !!!

A PLAN WITH SOME THOUGHT IN IT

WHAT!!?
WHAAAAI!?
IF YOU'RE GONNA DO THAT, THEN JUST TELL HIM ALREADY!!!
THIS ISN'T A HIDDEN CAMERA SHOW!!
YOU'VE BEEN QUIET ALL THIS TIME FOR THAT? YOU TRYING TO MESS WITH US!?
YOU GOTTA GIVE IT A TWIST!!!
USE YOUR BRAIN!!!
HE TOTALLY FORGOT HE WAS TRYING TO STOP HER.

UHHH...
UMMM...
THEN...
...I'LL HAVE HIM COME OUT TO THE FRONT OF THE SCHOOL INSTEAD...
AND THEN...
...I'LL SEND HIM A TEXT...
PIROROOO (RIIIING)
ピロロー♪
WHAT...!?
YOU'RE CALLING THAT A TWIST...!?

WHEN HE LOOKS UP AT THE ROOF...
THAT'S SEO-SENPAI HOLDING A ROLL OF CLOTH...?
BA (FWOOSH)
!!
WH-WHAT'S WRITTEN ON IT...!?

My true identity...? Rearrange the 7 letters.
LALOERI
WHY DID YOU MAKE THAT PART THE TWIST!!?

BUT I JUST DID WHAT YOU SAID

WHAT? THAT'S NOT HOW I SHOULD DO IT?
I JUST DID WHAT YOU SAID.
BOO...
BOO...
NOT LIKE THAT...
THINK ...HOW ... DOES THE SCENE GO IN A SHOUJO MANGA WHEN SOMEONE REVEALS THEIR SECRET ...?

THAT'S IT ...!!!
IT'S REALLY COMMON FOR THE PERSON TO TELL THEIR SECRET WHEN THEY'RE PROTECT-ING THE OTHER!!!
I MADE IT IN TIME...
YOU'RE... PRINCESS KNIGHT. ..!!
WAIT. NO...
PARA (DROP)
SAKUMA-SAN...!!?
YOU FIGURED IT OUT...

I GET IT... THEN...
BA
WAKA! LOOK OUT!!!
SEO-SENPAI!?

GO (THUD)
I'm Lorelai!!
NOT LIKE THAT!
SA (FWISH)
JAAAN (TA-DAA)

THE SEO IN MY MIND

IT'S JUST NOT DRAMATIC AT ALL.
WAIT A MINUTE.
I'M GOING TO SIMULATE THINGS IN MY HEAD.
IF I USE ALL MY SHOUJO MANGA SKILLS, I CAN TURN EVEN SEO INTO A HEROINE.
FOR EXAMPLE...

WAKA'S SURROUNDED BY DELINQUENTS ...!!!
OH NO ...!!!
SUU (INHALE)
I MIGHT END UP REVEALING MY SECRET ...
...BUT PLEASE ...!!!
LET MY SONG PUT EVERYONE TO SLEEP ...!!!

GUSHA (CRUMPLE)
HEY.
HE FELL ASLEEP.
REALLY?
HE'S WIDE-OPEN. LET'S GET HIM!

AH, AGH!
IT'S SO ONE-SIDED ...!!!
BIKU (FLINCH)
IT'S YOUR FAULT THAT WAKAMATSU ...!
BIKU
OH, HEY, SEO !!?
DON'T RUN AWAY, SEOOO !!!
WHAT'S GOING ON IN THERE ...?

APPARENTLY, HE'S THE WORST

I KNOW.
I DON'T KNOW IF IT'LL HELP OR NOT...
...BUT I ASKED WAKA ABOUT IT TOO.
IF SOMEONE HAD TO TELL YOU A HUGE SECRET, HOW WOULD YOU WANT IT DONE?
HUH...?
YOU ASKED HIM DIRECTLY!!?
THAT'S AMAZING!!!
IT WON'T JUST HELP—THAT'S YOUR ANSWER!!!

WELL, AND THEN...
THEN...
...I'D WANT TO HEAR GOOD NEWS AND BAD NEWS...
...AT THE SAME TIME.
TO BALANCE THEM OUT.
...THAT'S WHAT HE SAID.

JAAAAAN (TA-DAAA)
SO I JUST HAVE TO BRING BOTH OF THESE OUT AT THE SAME TIME, RIGHT?
I'm Lorelai!!
Taguchi-sensei is getting married!!
IT FEELS LIKE ONE OF THESE DOESN'T REALLY HAVE ANYTHING TO DO WITH HIM...
IT IS GOOD NEWS, THOUGH...

JAAAAAN
THEN THIS ONE.
I'm Lorelai!!
Someone cut your shoelaces!!
WAIT A MINUTE!!!
THE MARRIAGE WAS THE BAD NEWS!!?

IS TAGUCHI-SENSEI ALL RIGHT!?

IT'S HARD

LATELY ... ...SEO-SENPAI HAS BEEN...
...ACTING KINDA WEIRD...

SHE KEEPS GLANCING AT ME.
CHIRA ちら
ちら CHIRA (GLANCE)
SHE'LL LOOK LIKE SHE'S GONNA SAY SOME-THING BUT THEN STOPS.
UH... NO, NEVER MIND.
AND SHE'S BEEN CARRYING AROUND THIS THING, LIKE A PIECE OF WOOD?

I WONDER IF SHE'S ...
I'D LIKE A COF-FEE...
... PLANNING ON PLAYING A PRANK ON ME.
...AS PART OF THE TIRAMISU SET.
WHAT DO YOU THINK ...?

WELL, FIRST, CAN YOU NOT STICK YOUR ORDER IN THE MIDDLE OF THE CONVER-SATION LIKE THAT...?
IT MAKES THINGS HARD...

MY LITTLE SISTER'S MENTAL AGE

SO YOU SAY MY SISTER'S ACTING WEIRD...?

YEAH ...

SHE'S STARING AND LOOKS LIKE SHE WANTS TO SAY SOMETHING, HUH...?

......

ON BREAK

カッ
KA (FLASH)
SHE'S NOT GONNA CONFESS HER LOVE, IS SHE!!?
ちらっ
CHIRA
HAS EVEN YUZUKI FINALLY REACHED THAT AGE ...!!?
ちらっ
CHIRA

BUT WHAT'S WITH HER CARRYING A PIECE OF WOOD AROUND ...?
WANTS TO SAY SOMETHING
ちらっ
CHIRA
ちらっ
CHIRA
...SO MAYBE SHE...
PIECE OF WOOD

...TOOK IN A STRAY DOG AND WANTS TO BUILD IT A DOGHOUSE !?
SOMETHING HARD TO SAY
I WANT TO KEEP HIM IN SECRET.
YEAH, EVERYTHING FITS!
IT'S GOT TO BE THAT ...!!!
ARF!
ARF!
PIECES OF WOOD
SHE'S JUST LIKE A LITTLE BOY!!

GOT IT... A DOG-HOUSE, HUH ...?
HOW DO YOU BUILD ONE...?
SO HE REALLY DOES LIKE YUZUKI AFTER ALL ...!!!
HE'S GONNA DO IT FOR HER ...!?
SUCH A GOOD KID!!
I DON'T GET WHY, THOUGH!!!

HMMM...
FOR THIS ...
...IF I BORROW SOME TOOLS FROM HORI-SENPAI, I SHOULD BE ABLE TO MAKE IT...
GOTTA WRITE IT DOWN...
WHA—!?
YOU DON'T HAVE TO GET THAT SERIOUS ABOUT IT...!!!
IT MAKES ME FEEL BAD...!!!

NO!
I WANT TO MAKE IT PROP-ERLY!!
YUZUKI ...!!!
YOU'RE SO LUCKY TO HAVE SOMEONE THINK SO MUCH OF YOU...!!!

SO I WONDER WHAT TYPE OF DOG IT IS!
WAKU (EXCITED) わく
WAKU わく
WAKU わく
OH ...!!!
HE'S JUST A DOG-LOVER ...!!!

SHE'S JUST THAT OBLIVIOUS

AND THEN... ...THE DAY OF HER CONFESSION ARRIVED.
I CALLED WAKA TO COME HERE.
THERE.
I'm Lorelai!!
They're not carrying your favorite food at the store anymore.
AND I HAVE MY SIGNS READY TOO.
LET'S DO THIS!

BUT REALLY, THEY'RE WAY TOO WORKED UP OVER THIS...
THIS IS A HUGE CONFESSION, YOU KNOW!!
WHY AREN'T YOU NERVOUS!?
I'M JUST GONNA LET IT ALL OUT. NOTHING'S GONNA CHANGE.
GACHA (KACHAK)

HEY, WAKA!
SORRY TO KEEP YOU WAITING!
BATAN (SHUT)
OH.
SENPAI.
......
......
......

DO (WHOOSH)
NOW I'M GETTING NERVOUS.

YUZUKI SEO IS PANICKING!

NO WAY! I HAFTA JUST LET IT SLIP RIGHT OUT!!
DO (THUD)
DO
DO
DO
THERE'S NOTHING TO GET ALL SCARED ABOUT!!!

THIS IS WAKA WE'RE TALKING ABOUT. HE'S JUST GONNA SMILE NICELY AND ACCEPT IT!!!
HUH? REALLY?
?
AFTER ALL, I'M HIS BELOVED LORELAI-SAN!!!

HE MIGHT GET SHOCKED AND NEVER SMILE AT YOU EVER AGAIN...
DO
DO
DO
DO
DO
I-I-IT'S GONNA BE JUST FINE! HE'S GONNA SMILE AT ME!!!
A- ANYWAY ...

...I THINK I'LL LET HIM DOWN FIRST...
SU (FWISH)
They're not carrying your favorite food at the store anymore.
WHA—!!?
BUT THEY'RE SO GOOD!!!
THE HAMBURGER-STUFFED BUNS!?

SMILE AT ME WITH SPARKLY EYES

SO... ...ACTUALLY...

I- I'M... ...LORELAI...!!!

...SMILE... SMILE...!!!

SMILE...

OH, I SEE. YOU'RE LORELAI-SAN.
UNDERSTOOD.
SO... ...WHERE'S THE DOG?
..........HUH?
THE DOG?

BEFORE THE CONFESSION

GET SURPRISED!!
WHY!!?
I'M LORELAI! LORE-LAI!!!
I SAID I UNDER-STAND.
YOU'RE LORELAI-SAN.
GUOOO (ROOOAR)
WOW, AMAZING.

JUST KIDDING.
HEH HEH HEH!
IT'S ALL RIGHT.
EVEN IF YOU'RE NOT LORELAI-SAN...
...YOU CAN STILL ASK ME FOR A FAVOR.
COME ON!

I MADE YOU A DOG-HOUSE.
SO...
...WHERE'S THE DOG?
WAKU (EXCITED)
わく わく
WAKU

I CAN'T BE-LIEVE...
...YOU COULDN'T MAKE YOUR CONFES-SION AT ALL...
THAT WAS A SHOCK...
YOU'RE GONNA HAVE TO START BY BUILDING SOME TRUST BETWEEN YOU TWO.
GOOD LUCK!
......

MORE IN-DEPTH
SO... ...HOW IS THIS THE BAD NEWS ANYWAY...?
Taguchi-sensei is gettin mar
ISN'T IT A GOOD THING...?
TAGUCHI-SENSEI HAS THE WORST LUCK WITH MEN...
...SO EVERYONE'S SAYING THERE'S NO WAY THIS GUY IS A GOOD GUY.
IT MIGHT EVEN BE A SCAM.
O— OH...
BUT YOU'RE RIGHT.
WAKA MIGHT NOT KNOW ALL THAT, SO I SHOULD EXPLAIN IT A LITTLE MORE.
Taguchi-sensei has the worst luck with men, but she said...
..."Marry me."
She's definitely gonna regret that.
YOU'RE RIGHT. THAT'S A LOT EASIER TO UNDERSTAND.
MAYBE I SHOULD EXPLAIN ABOUT WAKA'S FAVORITE FOOD TOO.
Those hamburger-filled buns you really like...
...actually didn't sell...
...so they're discontinued.
YOU DON'T HAVE TO BE THAT SPECIFIC.
IT'S JUST MEAN.

[Extra]

WRONG ORDER

RE-VENGE
WAKA... HEAR ME OUT ONE MORE TIME.
IT'S REALLY IMPORTANT.
ガチャ GACHA (CLATTER)
ガチャ GACHA
ガチャ GACHA
IS IT JUST ME, OR ARE THERE MORE NOW?
THOSE SIGNS...

スッ SU (FWISH)
IT'S FINE—JUST LOOK AT THIS.
I'm Lorelai!!
...HAAH...
THAT'S ENOUGH OF THAT...

スッ SU
...actually didn't sell...
D—DIDN'T SELL...!!?
NO!
YOU DON'T HAVE TO PUT YOURSELF DOWN LIKE THAT...!!!
YOU'RE STILL YOUNG!!!

スッ SU
Marry me."
BWA...?
AM I... GETTING PRESSED INTO MARRIAGE RIGHT NOW...!!?

[ISSUE 103]

BRIGHT. SHINING SUN

OKAAY, WAKA!!!
LET'S CATCH A MOVIE ON THE WAY HOME TODAY!!
IT'S ALL GOOD!!
I'LL EVEN LET YOU PICK WHAT WE WATCH!!!

SHE'S DESPERATE TO GAIN HIS TRUST...
UH...I WANT TO SEE THAT ROMANTIC ONE THAT'S SHOWING RIGHT NOW...
UGH!
O-OKAY, LEAVE IT TO ME!!!
APPARENTLY, SHE'S WORKING FROM "THE NORTH WIND AND THE SUN."
WHERE KINDNESS WINS OVER THE TRAVELER.

さん SAN (SHINE)
さん SAN
さん SAN
Anything troubling you!? If there is, then tell me about it!!!
I'll do something to help!!!
I really care about you!!!
さん SAN
さん SAN
さん SAN

......
HEY.
THE TRAVELER IS WRAPPING HIS CLOAK UP.
YUZUKI...!!!

BUT YOU KNOW, I KINDA LIKE IT...
WAKA!!! WAKA!!! WAKA!!!
WHAT IS IT? GEEZ...
HUUUUH!!?

SOOO...?

S—
SO THAT MEANS...
...NOZAKI-KUN THINKS YUZUKI...
HE THINKS...
...THAT OF HER...!!?
GIRLS WHO GIVE THEIR ALL LIKE THAT...
...ARE REALLY CUTE... ♡

SEEING THE TABLES GET TURNED IS PRETTY FUN...
YOU CAN'T JUST DO WHAT-EVER YOU WANT!!!!
COME ON, BARK FOR ME!!
THIS IS THE...
...RE-VERSE OF THAT TIME...
YOU'RE...?
YOU'RE MY DOG!!!!
UGH...
HA-HA-HA-HA-HA!
OH HO HO HO!
SERVES YOU RIGHT!!!
OHHH...! LIKE THAT...
I LIKE THAT KIND OF THING.

WAIT A MINUTE.
SO HE THINKS SHE'S GETTING WHAT SHE DESERVES RIGHT NOW...?
SHE FOUND OUT.

A WONDERFUL CATHARSIS

I'M NOT REALLY SURE HOW I FEEL ABOUT MANGA WHERE YOU'RE SUPPOSED TO THINK "TAKE THAT!" ABOUT THE HERO, THOUGH...
ESPE-CIALLY WITH SHOUJO MANGA.
BUT IT HAS A NICE SENSE OF CATHAR-SIS.
WELL, GUESS IT'S BETTER THAN THEM STICKING TOGETHER AND ENDING UP HAPPY...

AS FOR THE PLOT...
...FIRST, YOU INTRO-DUCE THE DOWN-TRODDEN MAIN CHARAC-TER.
MY FIANCÉ IS WITH ANOTHER WOMAN AGAIN.
I DO...
...HIS WORK FOR HIM.
BUT HE'S THE ONLY ONE WHO GETS RECOGNI-TION FOR IT...
COME ON.
YOU'RE NOT DONE YET?
YOU'RE SO SLOW. HONESTLY, THIS IS SO SIMPLE.
U...
UUUUGH...!!!
CATHARSIS

FINALLY, SHE HITS HER LIMIT AND REMOVES HERSELF FROM THE SITUATION.
I CAN'T DO THIS ANY-MORE...
HE USED TO BE SO KIND, BUT...
I CAN'T KEEP GOING WITH JUST MEMORIES ANY-MORE...
SO I...
Fare-well...
...DISAP-PEARED FROM HIS LIFE.
SH-SHE DID IT...!!! SHE FINALLY DID IT...!!!
SHE RAN AWAY!!
CATHARSIS
SFX: ZUZUZU (WHOOSH)

AND THEN, YOU SEE THE MAN'S SIDE WHEN HE REALIZES EVERY-THING.
THIS DESIGN JUST WON'T DO.
THE OLD ONES WERE SO MUCH BETTER.
BUT I DREW THIS MYSELF...!!
WHA!?
YOU'VE JUST BEEN SO LAME LATELY!
BECAUSE SHE ALWAYS PICKED OUT MY CLOTHES FOR ME...!?
NO WAY...!
ARE YOU SAYING...
...THAT SHE WAS MORE TALENTED THAN ME...!?
MORE...!!!
SHOW ME MORE SCENES LIKE THIS...!!!
THEY'RE SO GREAT!!
CATHARSIS

POPULARITY RISING

WHAT HAPPENS AT THE END OF STORIES LIKE THIS?
BAD END FOR THE HERO?
WELL...
SOME-TIMES, A NEW GUY SHOWS UP...
...OR THE FIRST GUY HAS A CHANGE OF HEART.

WHAAAAI!?
SHE LETS IT SLIDE JUST BECAUSE HE HAS A CHANGE OF HEART!!?
THAT'S BECAUSE READERS TEND TO LIKE PEOPLE WHO WORK HARD.
MALE OR FEMALE, IT DOESN'T MATTER.
WHAAAAI!?
REALLY!?

WHEN HE HAS A CHANGE OF HEART, IT GOES LIKE THIS...
IT'S BEEN EIGHT YEARS...
I STOPPED FOOLING AROUND WITH WOMEN.
I WENT BACK TO THE BASICS AND RELEARNED DESIGN.
THAT'S RIGHT...
••DESIGN CONTEST
...MY ONLY CHANCE...
...TO SEE YOU AGAIN—
THIS WAS...

OH...
IT'S BEEN EIGHT YEARS...
...AND HE'S WORKED SO HARD...
YEAH...
HE'S NOT CHEATING ANYMORE...
YEAH... HE DID WORK REALLY HARD...
YEAH...!
THAT'S THE IDEAL READER REAC-TION...!!
AS A CREATOR, I'M HAPPY!!!

REALITY

AT MIYAKO'S HOUSE
ANYWAY, IT'S JUST SO NICE TO SEE HIM GET EVERYTHING BACK AFTER ALL THAT HARD WORK ...!!
ARE THERE MORE MANGA LIKE THAT?
HA HA HA.
GIRLS REALLY DO LIKE PEOPLE WHO WORK HARD.
THERE ARE PLENTY OF THEM, SO READ UP.

OH, THIS IS THE TYPE WHERE SHE GETS TOGETHER WITH A NEW GUY!!
I DIDN'T REALIZE THAT UNTIL THE END!!
KYA (SQUEAL)
KYA
......
LUCKY.
MIYAKO-SAN AND I CAN BOTH TELL WHO SHE'S GONNA END UP WITH RIGHT AWAY ...
IT GETS BORING.
HUH? IS THAT TRUE!?

FOR EXAMPLE—
THIS ONE'S THE EX.
EX
NEW
THIS IS THE NEW GUY.
EX
NEW
THIS ONE IS THE EX.
EX
NEW
AMAZING!!! HOW CAN YOU ALWAYS TELL!!?

BECAUSE THIS ONE'S MORE HAND-SOME.
IT'S NORMAL TO GO WITH THE HOT ONE.
SO IT'S ALL LOOKS IN THE END...
......

ADVANCED CONFUSION TECHNIQUES

YOU CAN ALWAYS TELL WHICH ONE THE ARTIST PUT MORE EFFORT INTO DRAWING.
THEY GET MORE LARGE PANELS AND COOL POSES...
NO WAY...AREN'T THERE EVER ANY STORIES THAT TRY TO SUBVERT THAT...?
...HMM?

MIYAKO-SAN, LOOK...
HUH ...?
OH... I CAN'T TELL ...!
WOW!!
!!
SO THERE REALLY ARE SOME ...!!!
EXCITING MANGA WHERE YOU CAN'T TELL UNTIL THE VERY END ...!!!

WOW... THEY'RE BOTH ON THE SAME LEVEL ...!!!
STOP TREATING HER LIKE AN OBJECT!
HA!
SHE'S MY SLAVE.
DIF-FEREN-TIATE THEM !!!

BUT LOOK— IF YOU KEEP READING ...
NII-SAN, BOTH OF YOU!!
DON'T YOU FEEL SORRY FOR HER!!?
I'M GOING TO MAKE HER HAPPY!!!
DON'T MAKE THIS MORE COMPLI-CATED !!!
WHOSE BROTHER ARE YOU ANYWAY!?

THE BETRAYAL BEFORE YOUR EYES

NOZAKI-KUN WILL NEVER BETRAY ME.
I'VE READ A WHOLE BUNCH OF THESE NOW...
...BUT I DON'T THINK THEY'RE GOING TO HELP IN REAL LIFE.
YOU REALLY THINK THAT?
BUT WHAT IF NOZAKI GOT HIMSELF A GIRL-FRIEND?
GAH!?

WHAT IF HE STARTED BRINGING HER WHEN HE HAS TO WORK?
I JUST WANT YOU HERE WITH ME.
THE OTHERS CAN DO THE WORK.
!!!

AND EVENTUALLY, THEY START FOOLING AROUND TO THE POINT WHERE IT'S SERIOUSLY IRRITATING...
I... ...CAN DO BETA!
YOU'RE SO GOOD!
PACHI PACHI (CLAP)
BECHO (SPLAT)
NO WAY...!?!
N—

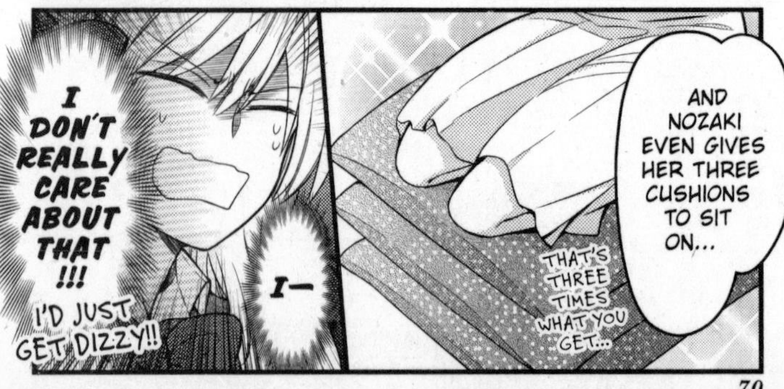
AND NOZAKI EVEN GIVES HER THREE CUSHIONS TO SIT ON...
THAT'S THREE TIMES WHAT YOU GET...
I—
I DON'T REALLY CARE ABOUT THAT!!!
I'D JUST GET DIZZY!!

SUDDEN BETRAYAL

THEN, ONE DAY, YOU JUST CAN'T TAKE IT ANYMORE, SO YOU RUN AWAY FROM NOZAKI.
Farewell...
POOR ME !!!

AFTER THAT, THE WORK JUST DOESN'T GO RIGHT BECAUSE YOU'RE NOT THERE.
I NEVER KNEW YOU WERE SO IMPORTANT ...
AND NOZAKI REALIZES JUST HOW IMPOR-TANT...
... SAKURA ...

HMM ...?
BUT NOZAKI CAN ACTUALLY DO BETA HIM-SELF...
I CAN DO IT.
SOME-ONE HE'D MISS IF THEY WERE GONE...
SOME-ONE HE'D MISS ...
UHH ...

I THINK IF HIS BACK-GROUND ARTIST LEFT, HE'D GO AFTER HIM WITH EVERY-THING HE HAD.
WAIT!!
BACK-GROUND
WITHOUT YOU...
BACK-GROUND
...I JUST CAN'T GO ON!!
!!!
HORI-SENPAI !!!

THE VETERAN SENPAI

I'M FEELING REALLY SAD RIGHT NOW...
...SO I THINK I'LL GO BUG HORI-SENPAI FOR A BIT...
TEKU
TEKU
TEKU (TRUDGE)
WHY HORI-SENPAI ...?

ばぁん!!
BAAN (SHOVE)
HORI-SENPAI!
CAN I TALK TO YOU!?
HUH? WHAT'S UP?
JUST CLOSE YOUR EYES AND IMAGINE SOMETHING FOR ME!!!

IMAGINE KASHIMA-KUN, WHO YOU DOTE ON ALL THE TIME...
...DECIDES TO BETRAY YOU!!!
HM ...!?
KASHIMA!?
YOU'VE DONE SO MUCH FOR HER, BUT SHE JUST DOESN'T GET IT...
IMAGINE WHAT THAT PAIN WOULD FEEL LIKE!!!

ARE YOU TALKING ABOUT LAST WEEK, WHEN KASHIMA SAID, "I HAVE A STOMACHACHE," AND WENT HOME, AND THEN I FOUND HER EATING CAKE?
OR RIGHT NOW, WHEN SHE PROMISED SHE'D COME READ THROUGH THE SCRIPT, BUT INSTEAD, SHE TOOK A NAP AND STILL ISN'T HERE?
OH NO. HE'S TOO USED TO BETRAYAL ...!!!

BETRAYAL AND JEALOUSY

NOT LIKE THAT!
SAY, FOR EXAMPLE, YOU DID KASHIMA-KUN'S MAKEUP, AND THEN SHE FOUND HERSELF A BOY-FRIEND!!
PLEASE GO OUT WITH ME!
OH...
AND THEN, EVERY TIME SHE GOES ON A DATE, SHE HAS YOU DO HER MAKEUP!!
I HAVE A DATE TODAY, SO DO YOUR THING!
Makeup
HOW ABOUT THAT!!?

UH...
OH ... UHH ...?
THIS ISN'T REGIS-TERING WITH HIM ...!!!

HMM ...
THEN SAY A NEW CLUB MEMBER JOINS WHO'S A REALLY GOOD ACTOR.
GOD OF THE STAGE!
AND HE'S ABLE TO MAKE KASHIMA SHINE EVEN MORE THAN YOU DO...
WOW ...!!
LET'S HAVE THOSE TWO ACT TOGETHER FROM NOW ON!!!

EEEK!!

AN UNBELIEVABLY SPECIAL SEAT

SAKURA'S IN A BAD MOOD. YOU NEED TO DO SOMETHING ABOUT IT.
SHE'S GONNA END UP CAUSING DAMAGE OVER HERE.
HUH!!?
WHAT SHOULD I DO...!?
JUST SPOIL HER OR MESS AROUND OR SOMETHING AND GET HER IN A BETTER MOOD.

HEY, SAKURA.
YOU GET A SPECIAL SEAT FOR LUNCH TODAY!
THREE CUSHIONS TO SIT ON!!
THE PART I DIDN'T REALLY CARE ABOUT CAME TRUE...!!!

OHH.
YOU DON'T WANT THAT...?
THEN...
...WANT TO SIT ON MY LAP?
JUST KIDDING!

SHE SAT THERE.

THE TRAVELER IS TREMBLING

...SO THAT'S WHAT HAP-PENED!
TEE HEE HEE!
MAYBE THIS MEANS WE'RE REEEEEEALLY CLOSE NOW...?
OHH? GOOD FOR YOU.
OH.
I'M GONNA GO PAY WAKA A VISIT.
GOTTA GET MY SUN TIME IN FOR THE DAY.

......
...MAYBE SEO-SENPAI...
...IS ACTUALLY TRYING TO BE NICE TO ME...
IF SHE IS, THEN I FEEL BAD...
HEY, WAKA!!
COME HERE! SIT!
OH, OKAY!

......
......
ZAWA (MUTTER)
ざわ
ZAWA
ざわ
ZAWA
ざわ

HER BULLY-ING...
...IS GETTING MORE MALI-CIOUS...!!!

NORMAL OPERATION

MAYBE I SHOULD GO TEASE KASHIMA A LITTLE TOO.

KA-SHIMA... I'M DONE LOOKING AFTER YOU ALL THE TIME.

HUH!!?

I'LL LOOK AFTER YOU, THEN!!

YAAAAY!!

HERE, SENPAI. YOUR TIE IS CROOKED.

LET'S HAVE SOME TEA.

HERE'S YOUR LUNCH.

......

THE NEXT PLAY...

...SHOULD BE ABOUT A BUTLER...

SO ANY-WAY...
[ISSUE 104]
FOR ONCE, I HAVE THE DAY OFF!
WHAT SHOULD I DO WHEN I GET HOME?
OH. YOU'RE NOT WORKING TODAY?
WANT TO GO SHOPPING, THEN?
YEAH, LET'S GO!
YAAY!
AND WE CAN GET SOMETHING TO EAT TOO...
OH.
WAIT A MINUTE.
OH... I CAN'T. TODAY...
...I HAVE PLANS WITH MY BOYFRIEND.
SORRY. I CAN'T JUST CANCEL ON HIM...
BWEH!!?
WAIT... UM... B-BOYFRIEND...!?
YOU HAVE ONE—!?

IT JUST HAPPENED, NATURALLY

WHY DIDN'T YOU TELL ME!!?
THIS IS THE FIRST I'VE HEARD OF IT!!
HUH...? IT'S NOT REALLY SOMETHING YOU HAVE TO TELL SOMEONE...
YES, IT IS!!!

A BOYFRIEND ISN'T SOMETHING YOU JUST COME ACROSS NATURALLY!!
HUH...!?
REALLY...!?
WHAT CAUSED IT!!?
HOW DID YOU MEET!?
WAS IT LOVE AT FIRST SIGHT!? A CLUB EVENT!?

WE MET...
...BECAUSE THE CAFETERIA'S MISO SOUP WAS REALLY BAD...
UM...
ISN'T THE MISO SOUP REALLY BAD TODAY...?
OH...
I WAS THINKING THE SAME THING...
IT'S REALLY BAD...
MISO SOUP!!?

AND THEN, WELL...
WE JUST SORTA ENDED UP GOING OUT, NATURALLY...
NATURALLY...!!?
AFTER STARTING LIKE THAT...
...HOW DO YOU JUST NATURALLY START DATING...!!?
ALL YOU DID WAS EAT SOME MISO SOUP AND SAY WHAT YOU THOUGHT...!!

HER VIEWS OF LOVE

WHAT IS WITH YOU?
HOW WOULD WE HAVE HAD TO MEET FOR YOU TO ACCEPT IT?
OUT WITH IT.
HUH ...?
U-UMM ...

MAYBE IF HE PROTECTED YOU WHEN THE SHELLS IN THE MISO SOUP SUDDENLY ATTACKED YOU...
PYU (SPURT)
ピュッ
PYU
ピュッ
ATHLETIC
WATCH OUT!!!
IT'S HOT!!!
KYA!
YOU'D ONLY REMEMBER THE SHELLS AFTER THAT!
NEVER MIND THE GUY!

OR IF THERE WAS A STRANGE DRUG IN THE MISO SOUP...!
ARE YOU ALL RIGHT!?
SCIENTIFIC
UGH ...!
THIS MISO SOUP ...!!!
IF THAT HAPPENED NOWADAYS, THE HEALTH INSPEC-TOR WOULD'VE GOTTEN INVOLVED, AND IT'D TURN INTO A HUGE FIASCO!
THE CAFETERIA WOULD DEFINITELY BE SHUT DOWN.

THEN WHAT IF A MYSTERI-OUS FAIRY CAME OUT OF THE MISO SOUP...!?
I KNOW ...
...THE MAN WHO'S MEANT FOR YOU! ♡
WHY CAN'T YOU LET GO OF THE MISO SOUP PART!!?
WHO CARES ABOUT IT!!?

IMAGE CHANGE

OH! HINA-CHAN!
OH. SPEAK OF THE DEVIL...
THAT'S MY BOY-FRIEND.
!!!
HE'S ...!!!

THIS IS BAD ...!!!
I KEEP SEEING MISO SOUP BEHIND HIM ...!!!

EH!? WE DIDN'T MEET BECAUSE OF MISO SOUP!
NO WAY.
HUH!? REALLY!?
GEEZ! REALLY, HINA-CHAN!
I KNEW IT!
STILL ...
...I JUST CAN'T STOP SEEING THE MISO SOUP ...

IT WAS CORN POTAGE.
IT WAS SO BAD.
Oh, he seems so Western.

HEAVEN AND HELL ARE BUSY

MAYBE EVERYONE IS DATING BUT NOT LETTING ON THAT THEY ARE ...
RYOUSUKE-KUN, DO YOU HAVE A GIRLFRIEND?
GAH !!?

WAIT— DOES SHE MEAN ...
...SHE LIKES ME ...!!?
N— N-N-N—
NO, I DON'T !!!

Really ...!?
PAA (SHINE)
SHE LOOKS REALLY HAPPY ...!!
I MUST BE RIGHT ...!!!

LET'S ALWAYS BE FRIENDS, OKAY!!?
MY COMRADE!!
KYU (SQUEEZE)
HER HANDS ARE SO WARM ...!!!
UGH ...!
BUT... NO WAY !!!

WE GET EACH OTHER

OH, SO HISAKAWA HAS A BOY-FRIEND ...
I GUESS I DO FEEL LIKE I'VE BEEN LEFT BEHIND...
Y—
YOU UNDER-STAND HOW I FEEL!?
WHAT IS THIS COMPLICATED FEELING!?

STILL, I'D UNDERSTAND BETTER IF SHE WERE REACTING MORE INNOCENTLY ...
UM...WHERE DO YOU WANT TO GO TODAY...?
MOJI (FIDGET) もじ
MOJI もじ
BUT LOOK!!
I WANT TO GO LOOK AT SOME CLOTHES TODAY.
OKAY!
LOOK AT HOW NATU-RAL SHE IS!!!
WHEN DID THEY START DATING ANYWAY!!?

MIYA-KO...
OH...
SHE'S PRETTY CLOSE TO HISA-KAWA ...
...SO IT'S A SHOCK SHE DIDN'T TALK TO HER ABOUT IT...
じーっ JI (STARE)
I REALLY DO GET ...
... HOW YOU FEEL ...!!!
......

I WANT SOME CORN POTAGE ...
WHY!?

TALKING ABOUT MANGA

WHAT DOES IT MEAN TO START DATING NATURALLY...?
UHH.
I GUESS THEY WERE TALKING LIKE USUAL...
...AND THEN WERE LIKE, "MAYBE WE SHOULD GO OUT OR SOMETHING?"...?
コンポタ

CAN: CORN POTAGE

OH, OKAY.
SO THEY'RE THE SIMPLE, DETACHED TYPE...
YOU THINK...
...WE SHOULD GO OUT?
...
I'M FINE WITH THAT.
THAT'S NOT MY STYLE, THOUGH...
STYLE?
YOU MEAN THAT'S NOT HOW YOU WANT THINGS...?

NO...
I WISH I COULD DO THINGS IN A CALM, COOL WAY...
THE SIMPLE EXCITEMENT OF THE EVERYDAY...
CONFESSIONS THAT JUST SPILL OUT OF YOU...
HUH...!?
SO SHE DOES WANT SOMEONE TO CONFESS THEIR FEELINGS TO HER LIKE THAT...!!?
FOR ME...

...CONFESSIONS USUALLY HAPPEN IN LIFE-AND-DEATH SITUATIONS...
YOU...
...HAVE TO GET OUT OF HERE!!!
I'VE... ALWAYS LOVED YOU...
LIFE...
WHA—!?
LIFE-AND-DEATH...!!?

SMALL TALK AND NATURAL CONFESSIONS

I WONDER WHAT NATURAL CONFES-SIONS ARE ACTUALLY LIKE...
WOULD IT FEEL GOOD?
WOULD IT BE EXCITING?
I DUN-NO...
I HAVE NO CLUE...
...ALL RIGHT.

LET'S DO IT.
HUH !!?
DO WHAT!?

WHOEVER CAN INITIATE A DATE WITH THE MOST NATURAL CONFESSION IS THE WINNER, RYOUSUKE-KUN.
A COMPE-TITION!!?
ME M— !!?
TH— THIS IS WAY TOO SUDDEN ...!!!
FOCUS ON MAK-ING THE CONVER-SATION FEEL NATURAL, OKAY?
AND START !!

NIKO' (SMILE)
... Hey ... ... have you heard, Ryou-suke-kun?
Love is all the rage these days...
THAT'S TO-TALLY UNNAT-URAL !!!

HIS EXPECTATIONS

I JUST CAN'T ...!!!
I'VE BEEN FOLLOW-ING THIS ROUTINE FOR YEARS NOW ...!!!
INTRO-DUCE THE TOPIC
THEME
THINGS HEAT UP
I HAVE TO START BY INTRO-DUCING THE TOPIC!!!
ROUTINE?
COME ON, JUST CALM DOWN, MIYAKO ...

I KNOW— HOW 'BOUT WE HEAD OUT FOR A BIT?
HUH ...?
WELL, HISAKAWA AND HER BOYFRIEND WERE GONNA GO SHOPPING.
LET'S GO DO THAT TOO.

YOU'RE AMAZ-ING, RYOU-SUKE-KUN.
IN AN ENTIRELY NATURAL WAY, YOU PULLED ME INTO YOUR PACE...
YOU'RE SO COM-POSED ...
WHAT KIND OF PLAN DO YOU HAVE IN MIND...?

OKAY !!!
IT'S A DATE !!!
HE HAS NO PLAN.

A FIRST FOR THE HONOR STUDENT

A CLOTHING STORE...
IN THAT CASE...
WHAT ABOUT THIS ONE?
THAT DOESN'T LOOK GOOD ON YOU!!!
WHOA!
YOU SHOULD... ...GO WITH THIS!
OH! THAT'S CUTE!
WILL YOU PICK OUT MY CLOTHES EVERY DAY IF WE START DATING?
JUST KIDDING!
OH, SURE!
I CAN START DOING THAT TOMORROW.
WHA...?
THAT'S IT...!!!
YES...!!!

RYOUSUKE-KUN...
...WOULD THIS LOOK GOOD ON ME?
HMMM.
I WON'T KNOW FOR SURE UNTIL I SEE YOU IN IT, SO YOU SHOULD TRY IT ON.
YOU MIGHT BE ABLE TO PULL IT OFF.
ACK!!?

UMMM...
I'D REALLY LIKE IT IF YOU PICKED OUT SOME CLOTHES FOR MEEE!
OH!
I KNOW SOMEONE WHO WORKS AT THIS STORE. I'LL HAVE HER PICK SOMETHING FOR YOU.
YOU'D RATHER HAVE A PRO DO IT, RIGHT?
UGH!!?

OH, THERE SHE IS. LONG TIME NO SEE!
OH, WELCOME!
THIS CHARACTER ISN'T DOING WHAT I WANT HIM TO DO...
THIS HAS NEVER HAPPENED TO ME BEFORE...!!!

DISASTER IN PANEL 2

YOU KNOW, SHOPPING WITH YOU IS PRETTY NICE. I GET TO LOOK AROUND A BUNCH.
GOING WITH MY LITTLE SISTER IS AWFUL
HIS SISTER !!!
THAT'S RIGHT—THIS IS ...!!!
I'M JEALOUS OF YOUR SIS-TER!
HUH ?
WHY?!
I WANT ... TO BE WITH YOU MORE ...
IT'S SO NATURAL!!

HERE I GO !!!
MUST BE NICE...
I WISH ...
...I COULD BE YOUR SISTER.

GASHI (GRAB)
NO! YOU CAN'T BECOME YUZUKI!
LET'S SAY YOU DID MANAGE TO BECOME MY SISTER. EVEN THEN, NEVER BECOME YUZUKI!
PLEASE DON'T!
NO...UM, RYOU-SUKE-KUN, YOU'RE CLO—
RYOU-SUKE-KUN, YOU'RE SO CLOSE ...
TOO CLOSE !!!

LONG-HAIRED MAN'S DESPERATION

THAT WAS A SHOCK ...
ドキ ドキ
DOKI (BADUMP)
ドキ
DOKI
DOKI
WELL PLAYED, RYOU-SUKE-KUN.
YOU WORK FAST ...!!!
LONG-HAIRED CHARACTERS ARE TERRIFYING...
NII-CHAN.
NII-CHAN.
NII-CHAN.
I'M GONNA HAVE TO BE MORE ON POINT ...!!!

OH, LOOK AT THIS, RYOU-SUKE-KUN!
THIS HAIR CLIP IS SO CUTE!
... NAH ...
YOU'RE CUTE ENOUGH WITHOUT WEARING SOMETHING LIKE THAT.

OH, LOOK! DUMB-BELLS !!
MAYBE I SHOULD WORK OUT A LITTLE!!
... NAH ...
YOU'RE PRETTY JUST AS YOU ARE.

I...
...LIKE YOU JUST THE WAY YOU ARE.
E—
EEEK ...!!!

THE CONFESSION HE WANTS TO MAKE RIGHT NOW

R-RYOUSUKE-KUN!!! NO FAIR!!!
THE THEME IS A NATURAL CONFESSION!!!
SAYING IT LIKE THAT IS AGAINST THE RULES!!!
THAT DOESN'T COUNT!!!

A NATURAL CONFESSION...
A CONFESSION!!
DO YOU GET IT!!?
YEAH!!!
YEAH...
OKAY...
UHH...

MY SISTER...
...IS GOOD AT SPORTS, BUT...
...SHE'S A SELFISH BRAT...
...AND SHE'S BEEN BULLYING THIS BOY, WHO'S HER KOUHAI...

AND THE OTHER DAY...
...SHE TOOK IN A STRAY DOG...
WHAT'S WITH THIS CONFESSION...!!?

IT JUST HAPPENED, NATURALLY

...SO YOU TWO ...
...HAVE BEEN DOING STUPID STUFF LIKE THAT ALL THIS TIME?
PLAYING AT A NATURAL CONFESSION... THAT'S A NEW ONE...

BUT HOW'D HE END UP LIKE THAT...?
WAAAAAAAH!
PLEASE, MIYAKO! JUST DON'T BECOME LIKE MY SISTER !!
YOU'RE FINE JUST THE WAY YOU ARE, MIYAKO!!!
OH! ...
APPARENTLY, HIS LITTLE SISTER IS A BIT OF A HANDFUL...
HE'S REALLY LOUD, SO CAN YOU SHUT HIM UP?
HE'S RUINING THE BOOZE.

UMM...
Everything's okay, Ryousuke-kun. Don't worry.
I'm ...
...never going to your house...
...so I don't think I'll ever meet your sister...

M— MIYA-KOOO-OO!!!
GOOD!!!
...
... SHE ...
... JUST ...
...TURNED HIM DOWN COMPLETELY NATURALLY ...!!!
ZO (SHOCK)

OH!
WHAT ABOUT THIS !!?
THIS ISN'T LIKE YUZUKI AT ALL!!!
NOT IF YOU MAKE IT REALLY HIGH UP. SEE!!?
OHHH!
IF YOU DO IT THIS WAY, IT LOOKS REALLY GOOD!!!
HUH ...?
UM ...
IT REALLY SUITS YOU, MIYAKO! SO GREAT!!!
U-UM ...
TH-THEN I'LL GET TWO...

THE MYSTERIOUS SALES PITCH AND THE WOMAN WHO CAN'T SAY NO

[Extra] COUPLE MOODS

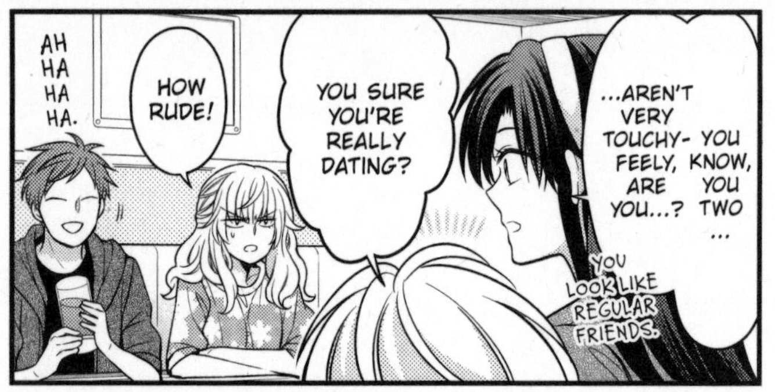
YOU KNOW, YOU TWO... ...AREN'T VERY TOUCHY-FEELY, ARE YOU...?
YOU LOOK LIKE REGULAR FRIENDS.
YOU SURE YOU'RE REALLY DATING?
HOW RUDE!
AH HA HA HA.

HAVE YOU SAID "I LOVE YOU!♡" YET?
HISAKAWA-SAN!
HA!
I WON'T GET FLUSTERED THAT EASILY, YOU KNOW!
SERIOUSLY, I LOVE YOU. I LOVE YOU. I TOTALLY LOVE YOU! ♡
HO-HO-HO-HO-HO!

WAIT—HAVE YOU NOT ACTU-ALLY SAID IT YET!!?
WHAA—!?
WHAT THE HELL HAVE YOU BEEN DOING!!?
DON'T GET ALL BITTERSWEET ON US NOW!!!

[ISSUE 105]
RED BEAN BREAD
MILK
パー
攻
PERFECT CAPTURE
Otome Ga

BIRDS OF A FEATHER

PINPOON (DING-DONG)
Yes?
OH! NOZAKI-KUN, IT'S SAKURA!
Hm? Today's not a work day, you know.
I'M DOING MY DRAFT.
REALLY !!?
IS THAT TRUE!?

WELL, SINCE YOU'RE HERE, YOU MIGHT AS WELL COME IN.
......
I'M USUALLY HERE HELPING WITH SOMEONE ELSE, BUT THIS TIME, IT'S JUST ME ...
SO TODAY ...
...IT'S JUST ME AND NOZAKI-KUN ...!!?

HMM? OH, IT'S SAKU-RA.
DID YOU GET THE WRONG DAY TOO?
HA-HA-HA-HA-HA!
WE'RE SO ALIKE!
BIRDS OF A FEATHER!!

THERE'S NO NEED FOR THERE TO BE TWO PEOPLE LIKE THIS, MIKORIN ...
I'M GETTING ERASED ...!!!

THINGS HE'S HAPPY TO DO FOR THEM

ANY-WAY ...
...I'LL LET MAYU TAKE CARE OF THE REST.
KEEP THEM OCCUPIED.
WHAT?
MAYU-KUN!?
YOU'RE HERE!!?
DOING HOSPI-TALITY!?
CAN YOU REALLY DO THAT!!?

LEAVE IT TO ME.
SESE (ZOOM) せっ
SE せっ
A FUTON !!?
NO! WE'RE NOT GONNA SLEEP !!!
STOP IT!!!

SHUN (DROOP) しゅん...
......
Y— YOU ...WENT TO ALL THAT TROUBLE TO GET THEM OUT. SORRY !!!
Y— YEAH! LET'S DO SOMETHING THAT INVOLVES US BEING AWAKE!!
OKAY!!?

BA (WHOOSH) ばっ
DON'T TRY TO PUT US IN A HOLD !!!

CAN'T CHOOSE EITHER

OH YEAH, NII-SAN SAID THESE WERE FOR YOU.
GIFTS.
WHAT COULD THEY BE? ART SUP-PLIES?
?
?
UHH, THERE ARE TWO THINGS.

FIRST IS THIS.
どんっ
DON (BAM)
PLENTY OF DELICIOUSNESS!
どでかいチーズケーキ
LOTS TO EAT!!
GIANT CHEESECAKE
VERY SATISFYING!!
!!!
THAT'S FOR ME!!!
BUT IT'S REALLY HARD TO ADMIT THAT PACKAGE IS FOR ME...!!!

I-I JUST CAN'T TELL WHO THIS IS FOR ...!
LET'S EAT IT TO-GETH-ER!♡
TEE HEE HEE!
ばっ
BA (FWOOSH)
Silly!!!
PLENTY OF DELICIOUSNESS!
LOTS TO EAT!!
TEE-HEE-HEE!
HA-HA-HA-HA!
We can tell who gets which one if we look at the other one!!!
Come on, Mayu!!!
OKAY.
THE OTHER ONE...

CASE: OTOME GAME IKEMEN SYNDROME

...IS THIS.
スッ
SU (FWISH)
乙女向けゲーム
イケメンシンドローム

ADVICE FROM SOMEONE WHO'S ALREADY PLAYED IT

THEY DECIDED TO PLAY IT.
BUT WHY IS THIS FOR ME ...?
I'M PRETTY SURE THIS WAS MEANT FOR MIKO-RIN...
IT'S NOT FOR ME!!!
I THINK YOU SHOULD PLAY IT!!
I JUST LOVE CHEESE-CAKE!

U—
UMM, MIKO-RIN...
...WHAT AM I SUP-POSED TO DO NOW?
AGH!
IT'S NOT LIKE I KNOW ANYTHING ABOUT OTOME GAMES EITHER, YOU KNOW!!!

BASED ON THE CASE, IT LOOKS LIKE AN ADVEN-TURE GAME...
...SO I BET IT'S THE TYPE WHERE YOU MAKE CHOICES.
IT STARTS WITH A SHARED ROUTE THAT SPLITS UP, SO MAKE SURE YOU SAVE IN DIFFERENT SLOTS.
OH... HE DEFI-NITELY KNOWS A LOT ABOUT THIS GAME ...!!

IF THERE'S A FIELD DAY IN THE GAME, YOU NEED GOOD SPORTS SKILLS...
...SO I THINK YOU SHOULD RAISE THEM.
YOU CAN WIN.
WHAT IN THE WORLD IS HE TALKING ABOUT ...?

I KNOW NOTHING ABOUT IT

OH WOW !!!
A VIDEO STARTED PLAYING !!!
THAT'S THE OPENING MOVIE.
OHHH!
OH WOW, THE BACK-GROUNDS ARE SO PRETTY !!!
THEY'RE MOVING!!

WHO CARES ABOUT THE BACK-GROUND? LOOK AT THE GUYS.
THIS IS YOUR CHANCE TO DECIDE WHICH OF THE GUYS YOU WANNA GO FOR.
FIVE OF 'EM HAVE ALREADY GONE BY.
OH...
OKAY ...
SORRY.

Oh, he looks really cool!
That guy on the right !!!
See him, Miko-rin!?

HE DIDN'T GET ANY-WHERE NEAR AS MUCH SCREEN TIME AS THE REST OF THEM.
HE'S A SIDE CHARAC-TER.
YOU CAN'T GO FOR HIM.

A PRO AT THIS

The Brusque Author Nozomu Kurokawa
OH, THIS ONE I LIKE HIM!!!
HE REMINDS ME OF NOZAKI-KUN!!!

OKAY, SO, TO GET HIM, YOU BASICALLY ACT LIKE A STALKER.
KEEP GOING AFTER HIM.
YOU HAVE A KNACK FOR IT, RIGHT?
YEAH!

OKAY.
THEN FIRST, MEMO-RIZE HIS PRO-FILE!!
Nozomu Kurokawa
Character Profile
--- 0/X
--- Type A
--- Black
I SEE.
SO HE HAS FOUR PEOPLE IN HIS FAMILY...
OKAY, OKAY.
NAH.
THE ONLY STUFF THAT MATTERS IN THE GAME ITSELF IS STUFF LIKE HIS BIRTHDAY AND THE THINGS HE LIKES...
YOU DON'T NEED TO READ IT THAT THOROUGHLY...

HE LIKES "QUIET PLACES."
SO THAT MEANS HERE OR HERE...
IF I HAVE TO STAY A LONG TIME, THEN IT'D BE MORE NATURAL TO DO IT HERE.
In-Game Map
STOP!!! DON'T BRING THE REAL WORLD INTO THIS!!!
IT'S NOT THAT SORT OF GAME!!!

EVERYTHING SHE CAN GET

OH, MIKORIN, I HAVE TO MAKE A CHOICE!!
WHAT IS THIS?=
Where should I go?
Library
Museum
Department Store
OH, HERE... IF YOU PICK THE RIGHT ONE, YOU'LL RUN INTO HIM.
IF YOU GET IT WRONG, YOU'LL ONLY GET TO HEAR SOME GOSSIP.
So, he...
Hey!

PIRON (JINGLE)
LIBRARY
Kurokawa
Oh, it's you...
OHHH !!!
THAT'S GREAT !!!
YOU GOT IT FIRST TRY!!

PI (BEEP)
Loading...
Loading...
HUH !?
BUT WHY !!?
JUST KEEP GOING!!!

BUT THERE'S GOSSIP, RIGHT !!?
I HAVE TO HEAR IT ALL BEFORE I GO THERE !!!
YOU'RE WAY TOO THOR-OUGH. IT'S SCARY!!!
I NEED ALL THE INFORMATION FOR MYSELF...!!

SAKURA AND THE OTOME GAME

ON THE INDIVIDUAL ROUTE

Okay, fine...

I made some tea, so you can have some.

Kurokawa

Okay, fine...

OH WOW!!!

THAT SOUNDS LIKE SOMETHING NOZAKI-KUN WOULD SAY!!!

When I look at you, I feel like I could write an entire book.
WAAAAH!
I CAN'T HELP BUT SMIIIIILE.
SHE'S REALLY GETTING INTO THIS...
GIRLS REALLY DO LIKE THIS SORT OF GAME...

DURING A ROMANCE EVENT
Sleeping defenselessly in a place like this...?
You won't complain if I kiss you now, will you?
Kurokawa
Sleeping defenselessly in a
WHA—?
WHAAAAAAAAAAI!!?

THAT'S NOT RIGHT!!
IF SOMEONE'S SLEEPING, HE'S SUPPOSED TO GET A PILLOW AND BLANKET, ISN'T HE!?
SO (SLIDE)
Loading.
THIS IS JUST WEIRD! I'M DOING IT OVER!!
HER SENSE OF ROMANCE IS TOTALLY SCREWED UP...

TIME AND UNDERSTANDING

You... read my book, didn't you...?

...What did you think?

It was really interesting, just like always.

Something seemed a little off.

You're a genius!! It was amazing!!

...FEED-BACK FOR AN AUTHOR WITH A FEW WORRIES...
WHAT DO YOU THINK IS RIGHT?
PROB-ABLY THE MIDDLE ONE.
YEAH, YOU'RE RIGHT.
SOMETHING THAT'S NOT QUITE RIGHT THAT YOU NOTICED BECAUSE YOU'VE BEEN WATCHING HIM ALL THIS TIME...

CHIYO-SAN LOOKS COMPLETELY CONFIDENT ABOUT THIS.
YEAH...
SHOW US THE RESULTS OF ALL THE EXTRA TIME YOU SPENT STALKING!!

ピ
PI (BEEP)
You're a genius!! It was amazing!!
WHY!!?

THE RIGHT ANSWER

You're... mocking me, aren't you?
HUH!? I CAN ONLY CHOOSE THE ONE!?
I THOUGHT I COULD CHOOSE ANOTHER ONE AFTER THAT...
HUH!?
WHAT'RE YOU TALKING ABOUT ...?
GACHA (KACHAK)

SORRY TO BUG YOU WHEN YOU'RE HAVING FUN, BUT CAN YOU TAKE A LOOK AT MY ROUGH DRAFT?
OH, NOZAKI-KUN!!!
OF COURSE!!!
I'D LOVE TO READ IT!!

WOW!! I NEVER THOUGHT THIS WAS WHERE THE STORY WAS GOING AFTER LAST TIME!!
You're a genius!! It was amazing!!
THIS CHAPTER IS REALLY FUN, JUST LIKE ALWAYS !!
It was really interesting, just like always.

BUT IF I HAVE TO CRITIQUE SOMETHING, THIS SEEMS A LITTLE WEIRD HERE...
WHAT MAMIKO'S DOING...
Something seemed a little off.
SHE USED THEM ALL ...!!!

I KNOW

WRITERS ARE DELICATE CREA-TURES.
YOU CAN'T JUST SAY SOME-THING IS WRONG TO THEM.
SA-KURA... YOU...
...REALLY THOUGHT ABOUT THIS...
THAT'S A SURPRISE.

YEAH. GIVEN THIS STORY...
...THIS GUY MIGHT NOT REALLY BE A WRITER...
wa
I want you to be stricter with me about your opinions.
HE'S JUST TOO STOIC ABOUT IT...
TOO STOIC...

NOZAKI-KUN WOULD PROBABLY BE LIKE THIS.
Kurokawa
I want you to be nicer to me about your opinions! Praise me! Tell me it's interesting!!!
TOO PATHET-IC...

AND MIYAKO-SAN WOULD PROBABLY BE LIKE THIS.
Kurokawa
Getting feedback from others is bothersome for writers, so I'll think about it on my own!
THIS PERSON HAS PROB-LEMS...

TILL THE END

I DON'T THINK SHE'S GONNA GET ALL EXCITED OVER SOMETHING LIKE THIS...
POOR GIRL...
MIKOTO-SAN, LOOK.

CHIYO-SAN IS...

OOOOH!
HERE IT IS!!!
A REAL HEART-POUNDING MOMENT!!!
I THINK THIS IS THE LOVE CON-FESSION SCENE.
IT FINALLY HAP-PENED, RIGHT AT THE END!!!
Will you... stay with me...?

B— BOTTOM ... MIDDLE ... TOP...?
うろ URO (HESITATE)
I love you...!!
うろ URO
There's some-one else...
うろ URO
I can't.
THERE'S ONLY ONE POS-SIBLE CHOICE!!!

BUT I WANT TO SEE EVERYTHING ABOUT YOU

HE WAS JUST SO COOL DURING THE SECOND HALF!!!
KYAAAAA!!
THAT WAS SOOO EXCIT-ING!!!

THE CONFESSION SCENE!!
CAN I SEE THAT AGAIN? CAN I!?
KYAA!
KYAA!
SURE!! PLAY IT AS MUCH AS YOU WANT.

GOOD ...!!
EVEN SAKURA HAS A LITTLE BIT OF NORMAL EXCITE-MENT LEFT IN HER..
YOU'RE A REAL, PROPER MAIDEN, SAKURA ...!!!
Kurokawa
Will you... stay with me...?

PI (BEEP)
I love you...!!
There's some-one else...
I can't.
DON'T CHANGE THE DIA-LOGUE!

THAT GIRL IS HOPELESS

YOU KNOW...
I WONDER WHAT SORTA EVENTS WE MISSED IN THE SECOND HALF.
I'M GONNA LOOK IT UP.
UHHH. NO-ZOMU KURO-KAWA.
NO-ZOMU KURO-KAWA...

Nozomu Kurokawa route
Reviews
• The second half of his scenario is just awful.
• The writer obviously got bored writing this.
• This author has a tiny vocabulary.

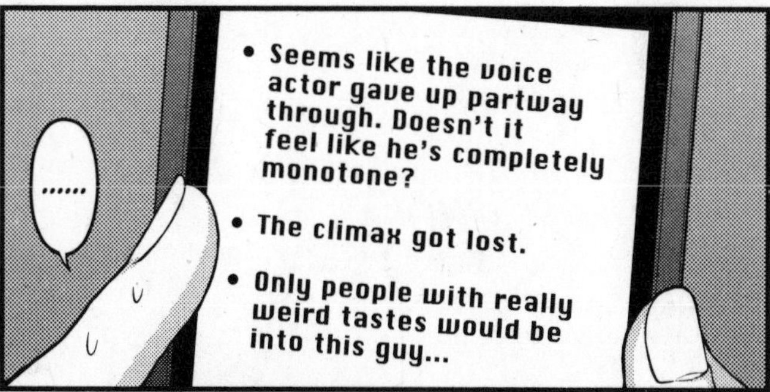

• Seems like the voice actor gave up partway through. Doesn't it feel like he's completely monotone?
• The climax got lost.
• Only people with really weird tastes would be into this guy...
......

YOU HAVE TO TAKE RESPONSI-BILITY FOR THIS!!!
GUH ...!!?
FOR WHAT!!?

[Extra]

THE GAME'S DARKNESS

WHAT !?
IT HAS BAD RE-VIEWS !!?
NO WAY !!!
BUT IT WAS SO GOOD !!!
KUROKAWA-KUN!!!

I REALLY LIKED HOW YOU GOT TO SEE HIS REAL PERSONAL-ITY THE FURTHER YOU GOT INTO THE STORY...
Kurokawa
I've been slacking off, even though my deadline is tomorrow.
ISN'T HE COM-PLETELY HOPELESS NOW...?

THE WAY HE ASKS YOU OUT ON DATES IS REALLY SIMPLE. I LIKE IT!
Kurokawa
I need some reference material, so let's go to the zoo.
DOESN'T HE JUST WANT THE REFERENCE MATERIAL ...?
THERE'S NO PASSION...

MY FAVORITE PART IS HOW HE ONLY COMPLAINS TO ME...
urokawa
I have to write scenarios for eight people in two weeks! This company is awful.
HEY!
SCENE WRITER !!!

[Extra]

A LITTLE EXTRA MAGIC

WAIT A MINUTE! THIS IS TOTALLY NOZAKI!!!
Oh.
Yeah.
That's good.
HE'S EVEN TALKING ALL MONOTONE!!!
N-N-N—
NO, HE ISN'T!!!!

CHARARARA (JINGLE)
AN EVENT BEGINS
Kurokawa
To be honest, I'm worried about something...
HEY, NOZAKI'S HAVING PROBLEMS.
C—
COME ON!!!
HONESTLY, MIKORIN!!!

Kurokawa
My ex-girlfriend said she wants to try getting back together...

KUROKAWA-KUN'S ROUTE IS KIND OF...
...AWFUL, ISN'T IT...?
THE SPELL'S BROKEN...!!!

[Extra]

SALES PITCH

ANYWAY, WHY DON'T WE TRY SOME OF THE OTHER CHARACTERS?
WHAT ABOUT THIS NICE-LOOKING SPORTS BOY?
NANA-HOSHI-KUN!!
AWW... A BASE-BALL PLAYER ...?
HMM. I'M NOT REALLY INTO THAT TYPE...

MAGAZINE: PERFECT CAPTURE GUIDE / OTOME GAME

YOU KNOW ...
...NII-SAN USED TO PLAY BASE-BALL.
Nana-hoshi-kun seems great!!!
NICE ONE, MAYU !!!

THIS AOTA-KUN IS REALLY INTO HIS SISTER ...
THAT'S KINDA WEIRD...
NII-SAN ...
...IS REALLY CLOSE TO OUR SISTER.
I'm kinda inter-ested in Aota-kun too!!!
AND WHAT ABOUT THIS GUY?
HE'S ...

CHIYO-SAN...
ACTU-ALLY, ALL OF THESE PEOPLE ARE JUST LIKE NII-SAN.
UHH.
THEY'RE ALL GUYS.
I RECOMMEND THEM ALL.
DON'T GET TIRED OF IT!!!

SAKIKO YUMENO-SENSEI BOOK SIGNING

[ISSUE 106]

Currently running in
Monthly Girls' Romance!
LET'S FALL IN LOVE ♥
NEW VOLUME ON SALE NOW!!

AFFECTING THE SERIES

KEN-SAN... ...WHY DON'T I...
...EVER GET ASKED TO DO ANY SIGNINGS ...?

......
DO YOU WANT TO DO ONE?
GAH!!?
I COULD IF I WANTED TO!!?
UH, WELL ... IT WOULD ACTUALLY HELP ON OUR END, BUT...

...IN YOUR CASE, HAVING A SIGNING WOULD PROBABLY AFFECT THE SERIES...
ガタッ
GATA (CLATTER)
AFFECT IT!!?
NO WAY... NO MATTER WHAT THE READERS SAY, MY WORK ISN'T GONNA CHANGE!!!

THOUGH, IF SOMEONE SAID, "CHANGE SUZUKI-KUN'S HAIR! ♡" I'D PROBABLY DO IT!!!
IT'S A HOT GUY 'DO.
AND IF SOMEONE SAID THEY REALLY LIKED THE SIDE CHARACTER RYUUNOSUKE-KUN...
...I'D PUT HIM IN AS MUCH AS THE MAIN CHARACTER!!!
YOU CALLED?
THAT'S DEFINITELY A CHANGE.

YOUNG NOZAKI'S SECRET PLAN

THAT ISN'T WHAT I MEANT. JUST LOOK AT THIS SELF-PORTRAIT.
Sakiko Yumeno
THIS IS WHO THEY WILL EXPECT...
...WHEN THEY COME TO THE SIGNING, YOU KNOW!!
My long-awaited high school debut!!
WHAT WILL THEY THINK!?
HAH!
I GOT IT ...!!

THEY'LL PROBABLY BE REALLY SURPRISED ...
...THAT SOMEONE AS BIG AS ME DRAWS ALL OF THIS...
IT'S SO EMBARRASSING.
SHE'S BIG...
SO BIG...
WHY ARE YOU ASSUMING THEY'LL BE FOOLED!?
IT'S NOT ABOUT YOUR SIZE.

DON'T WORRY. THEY WON'T REALIZE I'M A GUY.
IT'S OKAY. THEY WON'T.
OF COURSE THEY WILL!!!
HOW CAN YOU BE SO CONFIDENT ABOUT THAT!!?
DO YOU HAVE SOME SECRET PLAN!?

I'll have a sailor uniform ...
...tailor-made for me.
THAT WON'T BE ENOUGH!!!

THE IMAGES RUNNING THROUGH THEIR MINDS

IS IT REALLY THAT BAD IF EVERYONE FINDS OUT I'M A GUY?
?
WELL...
IT'S NOT THAT THERE'S A PROBLEM WITH THAT...
IT COULD BE A SELLING POINT FOR YOUR WORK.
BUT IN YOUR CASE, THE MAIN SUBJECT OF YOUR MANGA IS LOVE AND ROMANCE...

I'LL... WAIT FOR YOU...
I'LL ALWAYS BE WAITING FOR YOU ...!!!
MA-MIKO ...!!!
SUCH A SAD, DELICATE MAIDEN'S HEART ...!!!
AHH!
GASP!
...THAT GUY DREW THIS...
OH, BUT ...

MAGAZINE: ROMANCE

I'M NEVER ...
... TRUSTING MEN EVER AGAIN...!!!
SHE'S RIGHT ...
GUYS ARE JUST THE WORST !!!
WAH!
OH...
YUMENO-SENSEI'S ALSO A GUY...
SORRY.

Recent Happenings
Sakiko Yumeno
An adorable puppy got me right in the feels. ♡
COME ON!
HONESTLY, YUMENO-SENSEI!!
RIGHT IN THE FEELS... (CHEH).
KEN-SAN...!!! MY FANS ...!!!
MY FANS ARE MAKING FUN OF ME...!!!
I'M SO SAD!!

IT'S SO OBVIOUS

...ANYWAY... I WANT TO HAVE A SIGNING WHERE FANS DON'T ACTUALLY SEE ME...
...BUT CAN STILL ... ...FAWN OVER ME.
YOU GOTTA HIDE YOUR INTENTIONS BETTER...
AH-HA-HA-HA-HA!

WHY DON'T WE START BY JUST... ...SIMULATING A NORMAL SIGNING?
WE'LL COME UP WITH PLANS FROM THERE.
OH. THAT SOUNDS GOOD.

I REALLY LIKE READING YOUR MANGA, YUMENO-SENSEI!!
HA HA HA.
THANK YOU.
UM. COULD I SHAKE YOUR HAND?
HA HA HA.
OF COURSE.

CAN I HUG YOU!? CAN I TOUCH YOUR STOMACH!?
OH, PLEASE SIGN IT "TO CHIYO-CHAN♡"!
MAYBE "LOVE YOU, CHIYO-CHAN♡"!
YOU NEED TO HIDE YOUR INTENTIONS TOO!

ON THE TABLE DURING THE EVENT

WAIT.
WHAT ARE THESE DRAWINGS FOR?
HM?
IT'S A SIGNING, SO THERE'S GONNA BE FLOWERS, RIGHT?

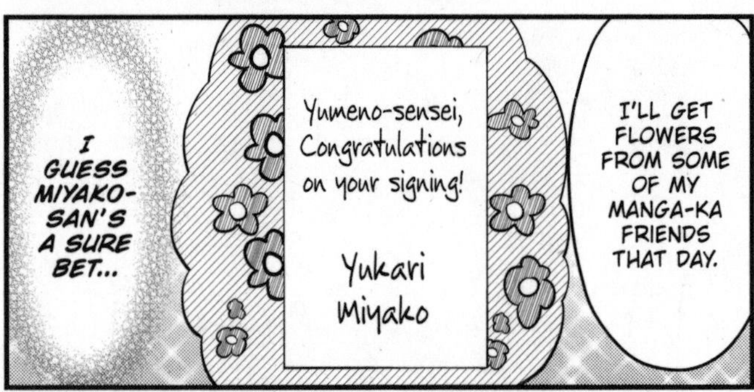
I'LL GET FLOWERS FROM SOME OF MY MANGA-KA FRIENDS THAT DAY.
Yumeno-sensei, Congratulations on your signing! Yukari Miyako
I GUESS MIYAKO-SAN'S A SURE BET...

AND I MIGHT GET SOME FROM MY ASSISTANTS TOO.
We love you, Sensei! ♡ Your assistants
HE'S INCLUDING ALL OF US IN THIS TOO...!!!

AND THESE ARE THE FLOWERS I'LL RECEIVE IN THE MORNING...
...FROM KEN-SAN.
AS A SURPRISE.
I'm so proud to be your editor, Yumeno-san. ♡ Ken Miyamae
THAT'S JUST PAINFUL...!!!

MY BOUQUET FOR YOU

ME TOO!! I'LL ...
... SEND YOU SOME FLOWERS TOO, JUST FROM ME!!
OH, OH, OHH!
REALLY !?
YEAH !!!
JUST WAIT A MINUTE !!!

SO... WHAT DO I WRITE ...?
Congratulations on your signing!
Someone who loves you♡
—BUT IF I WROTE THAT ...
...IT'D BE WAY TOO OBVIOUS.

HMM... MAYBE I SHOULD MAKE IT A LITTLE VAGUER...
I'm always watching over over you. ♡
Your number 1 fan
—HMMM ...
HE MIGHT NOT REALIZE THIS IS FROM ME...

きゅっ…
KYUU (SQUEEEAK)
I'm always watching you...
Red Ribbon Person
DON'T WRITE SOMETHING THAT SOUNDS LIKE THE PURPLE ROSE PERSON.

A HANDSOME SENSEI

I KNOW.
MIKOSHIBA, YOU SHOULD DO THE SIGNING FOR ME.
AS SAKIKO YUMENO.
HUH !?
WHY ME!?

MIKO-SHIBA ...
... YOU'RE GOOD-LOOKING ...
ZUI (LOOM)
O—
OH ...?
WHAT D'YOU THINK WILL HAPPEN IF THERE'S A HANDSOME GUY DRAWING SHOUJO MANGA?
EH ...?

IT'D PROBABLY BE LIKE THIS.
HUH...!? THERE'S A HOT GUY DRAWING SHOUJO MANGA...!?
WOW...
HE'S SO HOT...
...BUT HE'S STILL A NERD WHO SITS AT A DESK AND DRAWS OTHER PEOPLE'S LOVE STORIES...
GYUN (RISE)
GYUN
I DON'T WANT THEM LOOKING AT ME LIKE THAT!

WHY NOT? IT HAS ITS OWN APPEAL, YOU KNOW...
KYUN (COO)
HE'S HOT, BUT HE HAS SUCH A HORRIBLE FASHION SENSE...
ALL THE ACCESSO-RIES ARE SO LAME.
KYUN
HE RARELY CHANGES HIS HAIRSTYLE
...
KYUN
WHY ARE YOUR FANS ALL DISSING ME LIKE THAT...?

SCENE OF CONFUSION

COME ON.
JUST SIT DOWN AND TRY SIGNING A FEW AUTO-GRAPHS.
AWW ...
OH!
THEN I'LL PLAY ONE OF YOUR FANS!!
CAN YOU SIGN THIS?

Are you a fan?
You look so nervous, my adorable, little kitten.
If you give me a little mew...
...I'll sign your book for you.

S—
SAY SOME-THING !!!
DON'T JUST STARE !!!
IT—
IT'S NOT LIKE I'M EMBAR-RASSED OR ANY-THING!!!

THE MAIN CHARAC-TER IS DOING A SIGNING ...?
GEEZ!
DON'T JUST STARE AT ME LIKE THAT!!!
MAMIKO♡

SAY IT LIKE NOZAKI

WAIT A MINUTE! WOULDN'T IT BE WAY MORE NATURAL TO HAVE A GIRL DO IT !!?
SA-KURA, YOU DO IT!!!
HUH !!?
ME !!?

OHH!
THAT'S GREAT, SAKURA. YOU LOOK LIKE A HIGH SCHOOL MANGA-KA!!
NICE AND INNOCENT LOOKING!
ALL RIGHT!
NOW DO YOUR BEST NOZAKI, AND LET'S SIGN SOME AUTO-GRAPHS!!

YUMENO-SENSEI!
I'M A HUGE FAN!!
GIKU (CREAK)
OH!
YES !!!
THANK YOU!!
I LOVE SUZUKI-KUN! HE'S JUST SO COOL!♡
SHAKU (QUIVER)
OH, SUZU-KI!!?
UMM, YES!

I GET MADE FUN OF FOR IT SOME-TIMES, BUT I ACTUALLY REALLY LIKE HIS FACE.
IT'S EASY TO DRAW.
THAT'S DEFI-NITELY LIKE NOZAKI !!!

A MATURE REACTION

WAIT—A MANGA-KA CAN'T JUST SAY SOMETHING LIKE THAT!!!
HE'S STILL THE HERO. NO BASHING HIM!!
BUT B— WHAT SHOULD I DO...?
YOU GOTTA ANSWER WITH SOMETHING MORE, YOU KNOW, MATURE!!!

TRYING IT AGAIN
LET'S FALL IN LOVE♡ IS SO INTERESTING!
Oh! Thank you very much!!
YEAH, YEAH. SHE'S REALLY DOING IT...

BUT THIS PANEL LAYOUT IS KIND OF HARD TO FOLLOW.
I— I'll keep that in mind ...
AND THIS FORESHADOWING'S JUST A LITTLE...
SERIOUSLY, WHY DO YOUR FANS KEEP NITPICKING EVERYTHING!!?
Ah ha ha. Well, that's ...

MY EDITOR IS RIGHT OVER HERE. YOU'LL HAVE TO ASK HIM ABOUT THAT.
SHE PASSED IT OFF TO KEN-SAN.

THE REAL AUTOGRAPH

BUT YOU KNOW...
...WE CAN'T REALLY HAVE A SAKIKO YUMENO SIGNING WHERE YOU DON'T GET AN AUTOGRAPH FROM THE ACTUAL ARTIST...
SO...

IF WE DO THIS...
...IT LOOKS TOTALLY NATURAL AND WORKS PERFECTLY, RIGHT?
TWO PEOPLE, ONE COAT.
IT'S TOTALLY UNNATURAL.

COME ON. IF WE DO THIS...
...I CAN EVEN DRAW THE FAN'S FAVORITE CHARACTER FOR THEM.
OH, I SEE.
I GUESS THE ACTUAL ARTIST CAN DO SOMETHING LIKE THAT...
THEN I WANT MAMIKO...

BOOK: ...LOVE♡

HERE.
THIS ISN'T ANY DIFFERENT THAN HAVING SAKURA DRAW IT.
REALLY.

THIS IS AGONIZING

THAT'S JUST BECAUSE I WASN'T USED TO IT!!
AGAIN! AGAIN!!
SAKA (SLIDE)
SAKA
SAKA
さか さか さか
DOSU (WHAM)
ドス
DOSU
ドス
OKAY, FINE! JUST STOP WRIGGLING AROUND!!
THEN I WANT THE SIDE CHARACTER KAEDE-CHAN!
IT'S REALLY CREEPY!!!

...... VOLUME 4...
BOSO (WHISPER)
ぼそ…
OR IS IT VOLUME 3...?
BOSO
ぼそ…
MOZO (WRIGGLE)
もぞ
MOZO
もぞ
THIS ONE ...?
MOZO
もぞ

THIS BLACK-HAIRED ONE ...?
BOSO
ぼそ
NO ...?
BOSO
ぼそ
MOZO
もぞ
MOZO
もぞ
OH THIS ... ...?
HOLD IT OPEN LIKE THAT FOR A BIT.
MOZO
もぞ

I REALLY LIKE KAEDE-CHAN TOO!♡
TEE-HEE-HEE!♡
THAT'S NOT FOOLING ANYONE.
DON'T CHEAT RIGHT IN FRONT OF PEOPLE!

WE'LL STAY LIKE THIS FOR A WHILE...

So are you really okay like that...?
KOSO (WHISPER)
I'm not!!!
We're way too close! My back's super-hot!
But, but, buuut ...!!!

CAN I...
...STAY LIKE THIS A LITTLE LONGER ...?
KATAN (CLATTER)
!
!!!
IT'S REALLY LAME LOOKING, BUT DON'T BLAME THAT, SAKURA !!!

ACTU-ALLY, I...
KATA
KATA (SHAKE)
KATA
... WANT TO STAY ...
...LIKE THIS A LITTLE LONGER TOO...
!!?
NO-ZAKI ...!!!
HUH!? THE RIGHT HAND IS NOZAKI, RIGHT?
NOZAKI ...!!! YOU'RE NOT REALLY GONNA ...!!?

SU (SLIDE)
I HAVE DESSERT ...
!!!
HE'S GONNA DO THE TWO PEOPLE, ONE COAT THING FOR REAL ...!!!
HOOPS!
THIS
GOOD!

I'LL NEVER LET IT SLIP

THE TWO PEOPLE, ONE COAT BIT WAS FUN.
...SO ...
べちょっ
BECHO (SQUELCH)
MORE TO THE RIGHT, NOZAKI-KUN!!!
RIGHT!!? NOT THE LEFT!?
IT'S NOZAKI-KUN'S RIGHT!!!
WHAT ARE YOU DOING?

ABOUT THE SIGNING ...
WE DECIDED IT REALLY DOES HAVE TO BE ME THERE IF WE DO ONE.
... WELL ...
...YES, OF COURSE IT DOES.
YOU CAN'T HAVE SOMEONE STAND IN FOR YOU.

I WANT TO BE HONEST WITH MY READERS.
YES... SO...
I'LL NEVER DO A SIGNING ...
NOT ONCE ...

SAKIKO YUMENO'S RECENT LIFE ♡
I'M NOT GOING TO GET A BOY-FRIEND ...
MANGA IS MY LOVE RIGHT NOW... ♡
I'M ACTUALLY REALLY POPULAR IN MY CLASS! ♡
I HAD TO TURN DOWN SEVENTEEN PEOPLE JUST THIS YEAR.
AH HA HA! ♡
WHAT PART OF THIS IS HONEST?

[Extra]

BENEATH THE SMILE

SOMETIMES, ANOTHER EDITOR WILL GO WITH A MANGA-KA TO A SIGNING TO HELP OUT.
HANA-MURA-SAN'S EDITOR IS MAENO ...
WILL THIS BE ALL RIGHT...?

HANA-MURA-SAN. ARE YOU PRACTICING YOUR SIGNA-TURE?
NO.
I'M GONNA MAKE A REPORT AFTER THE EVENT.
I'M COMING UP WITH IDEAS FOR THAT...
NIKO (SMILE)
NIKO
SHE SEEMS PRETTY GENTLE ...

THIS IS WHAT I HAVE SO FAR.
MAENO-SAN AND ME ⑬ THE SIGNING
THE DAY OF THE EVENT
MAENO'S NOT HERE...!!!
DON'T OVER-SLEEP, OKAY!? ☆
HEY! WHAT WAS THAT CALL LAST NIGHT FOR ANYWAY, YOU JERK!!?
SHE'S ABSO-LUTELY LIVID!!!

OH!
CAN I PUT YOU IN IT TOO?
M-SAN CAME WITH ME THIS TIME.
HANA-MURA-SAN. DO YOU WANT SOME-THING TO EAT?
MUST BE ROUGH TO GET HERE SO EARLY IN THE MORNING.
I HAVE COFFEE TOO.
IF YOU'RE INTERESTED.
OH NO! HE'S A TOTAL ANGEL!!
HER TRUE STORIES ARE PRETTY EXTREME.

[Extra] YOU REAP WHAT YOU SOW

NOW LET HANAMURA-SENSEI'S SIGNING BEGIN!!!
SIGNING
YAAY!

OH, IT'S MAENO-SAN!!!
I LOVE READING THE AFTER-WORDS !!!
THE "MAENO-SAN AND ME" SERIES!!
OH? THANKS!!
CAN I HAVE YOUR AUTOGRAPH TOO!!?
WHA—?

I went to a signing for both Maeno-san & Hanamura-sensei!!
DAN (THUD)
DAMMIT!!!
前野♡
MAENO
Hanamura
Thank you

MONTHLY
GIRLS'
NOZAKI
-KUN

[ISSUE 107]
What is hypnosis?
CD included
How to Hypnotize
STEP 1

FOR THE SAKE OF MANGA

WHAT ARE THOSE? NOZAKI-KUN.
OH.
THEY'RE BOOKS ON HYP-NOSIS.
I WAS THINKING ABOUT INCLUDING IT IN MY MANGA.
OHHH?
LIKE WHAT?

A STORY ABOUT WHETHER YOU CAN REALLY MAKE THE PERSON YOU LIKE FALL IN LOVE WITH YOU...
...BY HYPNOTIZING THEM.
MAKE ME YOUR GIRL-FRIEND!
OKAY.
WHOA!
THAT SOUNDS FUN!
....

I THINK I'LL READ UP ON THIS TOO.
THAT'S A HUGE HELP, SAKURA.
YEAH, YEAH.
IT'S ALL FOR YOUR MANGA.

YOU'RE GETTING SLEEPY.
VERY, VERY SLEEPY.
COME ON. IT'S FOR YOUR MANGA.
SO HURRY UP AND FALL ASLEEP.
COME ON!

HER CRUSH'S ORDERS

"YOU SHOULD SPEAK CALMLY IN A LOW VOICE"...
THIS SOUNDS LIKE A GOOD FIT FOR ME...
OHHH !?
WANT TO TRY IT ON ME, THEN!!?
ARE YOU SURE?

I WONDER WHAT SORT OF ORDERS HE'LL GIVE ME...
YOU'RE ...
... FALLING FOR ME.
...WHAT IF HE SAYS SOMETHING LIKE THAT !!?
KYAAAA!

YOU'RE GETTING HUNGRY.
YOU'RE GETTING ...
...VERY, VERY HUN-GRYYY.

YOUR STOMACH IS STARTING TO GRUMBLE.
UGH ...
GUGU (RUUUMBLE)
I WON'T FALL FOR THIS ...!!!

KASHIMA-KUN'S HONESTY

WHATCHA DOING, CHIYO-CHAN?
HYOKO (POP)
YOU HAVE A STOMACH-ACHE?
KASHIMA-KUN!!

THIS WILL DEFINITELY BE EASIER TO DO ON SOMEONE WHO'S A LITTLE MORE HONEST!!
RIGHT!!?
HONEST ... SHE'S HONEST ...?

HUH? WHAT !!?
IS THIS AN HON-EST KOU-HAI CON-TEST !?
ZUI (LEAN)
I'M WAY MORE HONEST THAN YOU, NOZAKI!!!
THEN I WON'T LOSE !!!
SHE'S GETTING COMPETITI-TIVE...

I WANTED TO EAT SOME ICE CREAM TODAY, SO I HONESTLY SKIPPED REHEARSAL.
I FELT LIKE HORI-SENPAI WAS GONNA GET MAD, SO I HONESTLY RAN AWAY!!!
YOU'RE AN AWFUL KOUHAI ...

MUTUAL TRUST

OHHH, HYPNO-SIS?
THAT SOUNDS FUN.
DO IT ON ME!
TO MAKE THE HYPNOSIS MORE SUCCESSFUL, IT'S IMPORTANT FOR THE SUBJECT TO TRUST THE HYPNOTIST...
GOT IT.
ROG-ER!!!
I TRUST YOU!

YOU'RE GETTING SLEEPY.
SO VERY SLEEPY.
ぐー
GUUU (ZZZ)
WOW!!! NOZAKI-KUN!!!
SHE'S ASLEEP!!!
IT'S A TOTAL SUCCESS!!!

...NO...
SHE MIGHT JUST BE PRETEND-ING TO SLEEP.
HE DOESN'T TRUST HER...!!!

ばた
BATA (RUSH)
YOU'RE AWAKE, AREN'T YOU, KA-SHIMA!!?
ずた
ZUTA (GRKK)
I CAN TELL YOU'RE TRYING TO TRICK ME!!
THERE'S NO WAY YOU'D GET HYPNOTIZED, IS THERE!?
ばた
BATA
NO-ZAKI-KUN!
YOU'RE GONNA WAKE HER UP!!!
JUST STOP!!!

A MELODY OVERFLOWING WITH CONFIDENCE

I KNOW.
SHE'S TONE-DEAF, SO LET'S HAVE HER SING SOME-THING.
SHE WOULD HATE THAT IF SHE WAS AWAKE.
YOU'RE GOOD AT SINGING.
YOU'RE VERY GOOD AT SINGING.

SU (FWISH)
SHE'S GOING TO SING !!?
SHE HATES SINGING, BUT SHE'S GONNA ANYWAY!!?
!!!
AND SHE LOOKS SO CONFIDENT!!!

...MAYBE THE ONLY THING SHE LACKED BEFORE ...
...WAS CONFI-DENCE ...
YEAH ...
I'M SURE WE'RE ABOUT TO HEAR HER TRUE SINGING VOICE...

A SHOUJO MANGA-ESQUE ♡ IDEA

LET'S HAVE HER STOP SINGING, AND TELL HER TO DO SOMETHING A LITTLE MORE ROMANTIC!!!

ROMANTIC...?

SOMETHING MORE SHOUJO MANGA-ESQUE.

"NEXT TIME YOU SEE HORI-SENPAI, HE'LL LOOK LIKE HE'S SHINING."

SOMETHING LIKE THAT!!!

LIKE THIS...?

LATELY...

...HORI-SENPAI LOOKS LIKE HE'S SHINING...

SENPAI... ...DO YOU HAVE A MINUTE?

IT'S SO... ...DARK IN HERE...

SENPAI...

YOU'RE BLINDING...

WHY IS HE ACTUALLY GIVING OFF LIGHT!!?

HE'S NOT SUPPOSED TO BE BLINDING!!!

IT'S JUST KINDA HARD FOR ME TO MAKE KASHIMA THE HEROINE...
REALLY HARD.
TH-THEN LET'S DO SOMETHING MORE STRAIGHT-FORWARD!!!
"NEXT TIME YOU SEE HORI-SENPAI, YOUR HEART WILL START POUNDING"!!!

LATELY... ...SENPAI...
...MAKES MY HEART POUND...
KASHIMAA!!!
KYAAA!
DOKI (BADUM)
MY HEART'S POUNDING...
NO...
MY HEART...
HAAH!
HAAH!
NOZAKI-KUN, YOU'RE MAKING HER A PERVERT!!!

HE GOT IT TOGETHER

WELL, LET'S TRY SETTING A SUGGESTION.
NEXT TIME YOU SEE HORI-SENPAI...
NOOOOO!!!
GIVEN WHAT I JUST SAW, YOU REALLY CAN'T DO THIS!!!

MANIPULATING PEOPLE'S EMOTIONS WITH HYPNOSIS IS JUST WRONG!!!
OH. THAT'S GOOD.
THAT'S THE SORT OF THING YOU'D SAY ON PAGE TWENTY-ONE OF A THIRTY-PAGE ONE-SHOT.
THIS...
...IS JUST WRONG...
WAAAAH! I TOTALLY GET IT!!!
21

JUST KIDDING.
CALM DOWN. I'M GOING TO STOP.
NOZAKI-KUN!!!
I JUST HAVE ONE MORE THING TO DO.
OH! YOU'RE GONNA MAKE SURE SHE'S OKAY!!
YOU'RE SO NICE, NOZAKI-KUN!!!

YOU'RE GONNA FORGET EVERYTHING THAT'S HAPPENED.
HE'S DESTROYING THE EVIDENCE.

SPEED HYPNOSIS

I'M STILL NOT SURE WHETHER SHE WAS ACTUALLY HYPNOTIZED OR NOT...
SHE JUST LEFT LIKE NORMAL.
SEE YOU!
HMM.
I THINK KASHIMA-KUN'S PRETTY SUGGESTIBLE.
BUT SOMEONE WHO'S EVEN MORE SUGGESTIBLE—
OH!

NOZAKI-SENPAI, SAKURA-SENPAI!
HELLO!!!
THERE HE IS.

OHHH!
THIS IS A BOOK ON HYPNOSIS!!
UHH, LET'S SEE.
"YOUR EYELIDS ARE GROWING HEAVY."
How to Hypnotize Someone

ウト…
UTO (DOZE)
YOU'RE KID-DING, RIGHT!!?

THE STRANGE SITUATION BEFORE THEM

WUH ......
YURA (SWAY) ゆら
WUH ......
YURA ゆら
How to Hypnotize Someone
EEEEK!
HE'S MOVING REALLY WEIRDLY !!!
SNAP OUT OF IT, WAKAMATSU-KUN!!! ANSWER ME!!!
WUH ......

WOOF!
How to Hypnotize Someone
!!?

OH, THIS IS ABOUT DOGS !!!
HE WAS LOOKING AT HOW TO MAKE SOMEONE A DOG!!!
WOOF!
How to suggest "You are a dog."
THEN ...
... COULD THIS BE...
...SELF-HYPNOSIS!!?

IT MUST BE SOMETHING LIKE THIS !!!
I CAN'T DEAL WITH THIS PAIN...
...ANYMORE...
YOU ...
...WILL FORGET OKAZAKI-KUN...
FORGET HIM.
FORGET HIM.
FORGET HIM.
DISAPPEAR FROM MY LIFE...
DON'T RUN FROM THIS, NOZAKI-KUN!!!
GET A GRIP!!!

THE FORM OF HIS TRANSFORMATION

WAAAAAH!
HE JUST RAN OFF SOME-WHERE!!!
WOOF!
WOOF!
WOOF!
HE REALLY IS A DOG!!!
WHAT SHOULD WE DO!!!?

DAA (DASH)
WHOA!
HE BROUGHT A BALL BACK!!!
HE'S A DOG!!

WOOF!
WOOF!
WOOF!
KORO (ROLL)
KORO
WHOA!
HE'S BEGGING FOR YOU TO THROW IT!!!
HE'S A DOG!!!

HUH...? THIS DOESN'T SEEM ALL THAT DIFFERENT FROM HOW HE USUALLY IS...
I'M JOGGING!
PASS!!
SENPAI, DO YOU WANNA SHOOT SOME HOOPS?
WE CAN JUST PASS THE BALL!

YUZUKI AND THE BARKING DOG

WHAT'S GOT YOU ALL WORKED UP, CHIYO?
IT'S CLUB TIME NOW.
YUZUKI !!!
WAKA-MATSU-KUN'S IN TROUBLE !!!
WAKA?

BARK! BARK!
BARK!
OH NO !!!
HE'S A WILD DOG RIGHT NOW ...!!!
HE MIGHT EVEN TRY TO BITE HER...!!!

BAR—!
SU (SSK)
THERE'S NOTHIN' SCARY.
THAT ...
...LOOKS LIKE A HEART-WARMING TRUST-BUILDING SCENE !!!
THERE'S NOTHING SCARY.

WERE YOU TRYIN' TO THREATEN ME JUST NOW?
GIRI (SQUEEZE)
WHINE!
WHINE!
YOU'RE NOT SCARY AT ALL!
YOU LOOKIN' DOWN ON ME?
NO !!!
IT'S NOT LIKE THAT, YUZUKI !!!

THE RATIONAL CLUB PRESIDENT

MEANWHILE, AT THE DRAMA CLUB
OH, HORI-CHAN! IT'S KASHIMA-KUN!!!
KASHIMA-KUN CAME BACK ON HER OWN!
ISN'T THAT GREAT!?

NO WAY... THAT WOULD NEVER HAPPEN.
SHE'S DEFINITELY UP TO SOMETHING.
LET YOUR GUARD DOWN, AND YOU LOSE.
WHA—!?
YOU FOR REAL?
THE OTHER DAY, SHE SAID SHE WAS GOING TO THE BATHROOM AND THEN NEVER CAME BACK.
THEN I SAW HER OUTSIDE PLAYING SOCCER.
大道具用

BOX: SCENERY

WELL—
IT'S NOT LIKE I'M GONNA BE SURPRISED BY ANYTHING SHE SAYS NOW...
HEY, KASHIMA!
OH.
UMM...

NICE TO MEET YOU!
AHH! ARE YOU A NEW CLUB MEMBER?
HORI-CHAN!!!
ZURU (SLIP)
GASHAN (CRASH)
GO (THUD)

NEXT TIME YOU SEE HORI-SENPAI...
YOU'RE GONNA FORGET EVERYTHING THAT'S HAPPENED.
BY THE WAY, THIS IS THE SUGGESTION KASHIMA'S UNDER!!!
WHINE
WHINE
AND HERE'S THE REST.

"HORI"?
I'VE NEVER SEEN YOU BEFORE.
NO WAY...
KA-SHIMAAA...!!
She forgot!! What in the world is going on!?
[ISSUE 108]

TROUBLE IN THE DRAMA CLUB

THIS IS BAD!!!
...FORGOT WHO HORI-CHAN IS!!!
KA-SHIMA-KUN...
GUH!!?
WHAT THE—!!?
KA-SHIMA-KUN, IS THAT TRUE!!?

UMM... SORRY...
I REALLY DON'T KNOW...

KA-SHIMA-KUN...
REALLY... THAT FACE.

I CAN'T TELL IF YOU'RE ACTING OR NOT!!!
UM...
IT'S TRUE...
IS IT TRUE!?
OR ARE WE ALL SUP-POSED TO PLAY ALONG AND FOOL HORI-KUN!?
WHICH ONE!!?
WHICH ONE!!?

HELLO AND NICE TO MEET YOU

UH... UM... YOU'RE... THE PRESIDENT?
HORI ... SEN-PAI?
WAH!
THIS IS JUST PAINFUL ...!!!
AHHH!
POOR HORI-CHAN ...!!!

... WHAT-EVER ...
FUI (FWIP)
CALL ME WHAT-EVER YOU WANT ...
WAAAH!
THEY GOT ALONG SO WELL...
...AND NOW THEY'RE ALL AWKWARD—!!!

THEN ...
...I'LL CALL YOU MASAYAN.
SINCE YOU'RE MASAYUKI.

YAY!
WHEN'S YOUR BIRTH-DAY, MASA-YAN?
I GOT THIS WHEN I WAS SHOPPING THE OTHER DAY.
OH.
WANT TO SHARE IT WITH ME?
IT'S REALLY GOOD!
HUH...? THEY'RE ALL... AWKWARD ...?
HER COM-MUNICATION SKILLS ARE JUST PLAIN WEIRD!!!

OUR RELATIONSHIP

ANY-WAY...
..SHE FORGOT EVERY-THING ABOUT ME AND JUST ME...
KA-SHIMA... DID YOU...
...REALLY THINK I WAS THAT ANNOYING ...?

WAS I TOO HARSH ON YOU? DID I STRESS YOU OUT TOO MUCH ...?
MASA-YAN.
WHERE AM I SUPPOSED TO STAND IN THIS SCENE?

SO YOU ERASED YOUR OWN MEMORIES TO BE FREE OF THE PAIN...?
HEY, HEY!
MASA-YAN!
CAN I USE THIS PAINT-BRUSH?
URO (HOVER)
WANT SOME CHOCO-LATE?
URO
I HAVE CANDY TOO.
URO

AAARGH!
STOP HOVERING AROUND ME!!!
YOU'RE DISTRACT-ING ME!
THEY'RE SO CLOSE...

A DIFFERENT EXPRESSION

BUT STILL, SOMETHING'S NOT THE SAME...
...WITH KASHIMA-KUN.
YEAH.
THERE'S A SORT OF DISTANCE TO HER SMILE.
SEN-PAAAI!!
THE USUAL

OH, LOOK!
SHE DOESN'T USUALLY MAKE THAT SORT OF FACE.
YEAH, YEAH.
IT'S SO CALM. IT'S KINDA WEIRD.

NOW SHE'S A LITTLE EMBARRASSED OVER BEING PRAISED!!
WHOA! SHE'S REALLY DIFFERENT FROM BEFORE!!
HORI-CHAN MUST BE IN SHOCK...

UGH...
GIRI (GRIND)
DON'T BE HAPPY ABOUT THIS, HORI-CHAN!!!
THIS IS THE TIME TO ACT SAD!!!

COME ON!!
WHAT'S WITH YOU? JUST 'COS SHE'S SHOWING YOU UNUSUAL EXPRES-SIONS!!?
AREN'T YOU SUPPOSED TO BE MORE HURT OVER THIS!?
JI (STARE)
?
HORI-CHAN!!!
DON'T JUST STARE AT HER!!!
...WAIT— IS IT ME, OR ARE HER EYES KIND OF DEAD TODAY...?

KASHIMA MANIA

UMM ...?
ARE... THEY?
?
MAYBE IT'S HARDER TO TELL BECAUSE SHE'S SMILING...
HEY, KASHIMA, CAN YOU BLANK OUT YOUR EXPRES-SION?

SU (FWISH)
OH... YOU'RE RIGHT.
THEY FEEL KINDA COLD 'COS THERE'S NO LIGHT IN THEM. BUT IT'S ALSO COOLER THAN USUAL...

UGH ...!
GIRII (GRIND)
HORI-CHAN, ENOUGH ALREADY!!!

A FALSE ACCUSATION

SO ... YOU ONLY FORGOT STUFF ABOUT HORI-SENPAI?
DO YOU HAVE ANY OTHER MISSING MEMORIES?
HMM.
NOW THAT I THINK ABOUT IT, I CAN'T REMEMBER TOO MUCH ABOUT ACTING...
OHHH—
THAT'S TOTALLY CONNECTED TO HORI-SENPAI.

AND ...
...I DON'T KNOW WHY I EVEN JOINED THE DRAMA CLUB...
WHY DID I START ACTING AGAIN?
OHHH—
WELL, SHE DID JOIN THE CLUB BECAUSE THE PRESIDENT RECRUITED HER.
YOU CAN BE A HERO!
REALLY?

...HM?
ACTUALLY, WHY DID I ENROLL IN THIS SCHOOL IN THE FIRST PLACE?
?
HUH!?
SINCE THEN!?
HE WAS IN YOUR LIFE THAT EARLY!!?
WHOOOOOA!
......
AND ...

I DON'T REMEMBER ANYTHING FROM BEFORE I WAS BORN UNTIL I WAS ABOUT TWO...!!
THAT EARLY!!?
THAT HAS NOTHING TO DO WITH HORI.

REI-SAMA'S GREAT DEDUCTION

OH MY!! ONEE-SAMA, YOU FORGOT HORI-SAMA!?
IS THAT SORT OF THING TRULY POSSIBLE!?

DID ANYTHING STRANGE HAPPEN BEFORE ALL OF THIS HAPPENED?
ANYTHING STRANGE...?
NOW THAT YOU MEN-TION IT...
...I THINK NOZAKI AND I WERE FOOLING AROUND WITH HYPNOSIS...
OH MY!!! WITH YUMENO-SENSEI!?

HYP-NO-SIS... I SEE!!!
I'VE WORKED OUT WHAT YUMENO-SENSEI WAS TRYING TO DO!!!
I'M SURE THIS WAS THE PLAN...
THIS...
KA-SHIMA!!!
WHO ARE YOU...?
AND THEN, THIS...
NO WAY!
DAM-MIT! IN THAT CASE...!!!
GATAN (CLATTER)

I'LL JUST HAVE TO...
...ASK YOUR BODY...
And then, this would happen...
THAT'S NOT IT.

REPROGRAMMING

STILL, YUMENO-SENSEI...
...I BELIEVE YOUR METHODS ARE SLIGHTLY FLAWED...
KIII (CREEEAK)
ONEE-SAMA...

SINCE ONEE-SAMA IS ACTING UNDER SUGGES-TION...
SU (BREATHE)
...I WILL REWRITE HER INSTRUCTIONS WITH SOMETHING BETTER.
YOU...

...WILL DO AS HORI-SAMA ORDERS.
YES. EX-ACTLY.
YOU WILL BE HIS SLAVE.
RATHER, YOU WILL BE HIS DOG.
ARF, ARF!

Yumeno-sensei...
I've altered your instructions for the better...♡
THIS IS BAD.

THEIR RELATIONSHIP

MORNING, HORI-CHAN.
IF KASHIMA-KUN'S STILL ACTING WEIRD TODAY, YOU'RE FINALLY GONNA GET TO THE BOTTOM OF IT, RIGHT?
NAH.
I KNOW THERE'S SOMETHING WRONG, BUT...
IT JUST DOESN'T FEEL LIKE AN ISSUE.
WELL...
SHE HASN'T REALLY CHANGED ALL THAT MUCH, SO I GUESS THAT MAKES SENSE.
YAY, MASA-YAN!

Y'KNOW, WHEN YOU THINK ABOUT IT, IT'S PRETTY AMAZING.
NO MATTER HOW MANY MEMORIES SHE LOSES, THEY STILL GET CLOSE AGAIN RIGHT AWAY...
THEY MUST HAVE A SPECIAL BOND BETWEEN THEM...

GOOD MORNING...
...HORI-SAMA.
SHE GOT EVEN MORE DISTANT!!!

MY NAME IS KASHIMA. I AM HERE TO OBEY YOUR, AND ONLY YOUR, EVERY ORDER.
OH, BUT HE'S SPECIAL...
WAIT A MINUTE! THAT'S NOT THE PROBLEM HERE!!!
WHAT IN THE WORLD IS SHE TALKING ABOUT!!?

THE SUGGESTION IS FIRMLY IN PLACE

THIS IS BAD, HORI-CHAN!!!
HER EYES ARE EVEN DEADER THAN YESTER-DAY!!!
YOU'RE RIGHT ...!!!
IT'S OBVIOUS THAT SOMETHING'S WRONG JUST FROM LOOKING AT HER!!!
DID YOU HIT YOUR HEAD, KASHIMA!!?

HORI-SAMA.
WHAT ARE YOUR ORDERS?
COME ON!
SNAP OUT OF IT, KA-SHIMA!!!
OPEN YOUR EYES!!!
WAAAH!!
UNTIL NOW, I KINDA THOUGHT YOU WERE JUST MESSING WITH US...
...BUT THIS IS SERI-OUS!!!
WHAT DO WE DO!!!?

SHALL I...
...CARRY YOUR BAG?
WAAAH!
STOP!!!
THEN...
...LET US HURRY TO SCHOOL.
WAAAH!
THIS ISN'T KASHIMA!!!
AT THIS RATE, WE WILL BE LATE, ARF.

KASHIMA'S ACTING WEIRD!

HEY, KA-SHIMA. YOU MESSING WITH US...?
YOU JUST SAID ARF, DIDN'T YOU...?
?
WHAT ARE YOUR ORDERS?
HUH ...? UHHH ...
THEN MAKE SURE YOU COME TO REHEARS-AL...

I'VE BEEN WAITING FOR YOU.
O—
OH ...
READING THROUGH THE SCRIPT?
I WOULD LOVE TO JOIN YOU.
OH ...
WHERE WOULD YOU LIKE THIS?
WELL ...
... OVER THERE ...

ARE YOU SERI-OUS!?
STOP GETTING USED TO IT SO FAST!!!
KASHIMA-KUN'S ACTING WEIRD!!!

LIKE IN A MANGA

I HEAR KASHIMA-KUN'S BEEN ACTING WEIRD!!!
MIKORIN INTEL
HUH !?
WEIRD!?
WHAT SHOULD WE DO ...!!?
SHE MIGHT STILL BE UNDER THE INFLUENCE OF THE HYPNOSIS...!!!
WE SHOULD GO CHECK!!!

WHAT DO WE DO...? WHAT IF THINGS BETWEEN THEM ...
...ARE AWKWARD, LIKE IN A MANGA, AND IT'S OUR FAULT ...!!?
KASHIMA!!!
WHO ARE YOU?
KASHIMA-KUN... HORI-SENPAI ...!!!

LIKE I SAID!
WHY DO YOU KEEP ACCEPTING IT!!?
だす DASU (STOMP)
だす DASU
EVEN IF YOU DON'T LOOK CLOSELY ...
...YOU KNOW SHE'S ACTING WEIRD!!
AND YOU NEED TO GET A GRIP, KASHIMA-KUN!!!
......
IT'S TRUE.

WAH!
THIS SITUATION ...
...IS JUST PLAIN WRONG !!!
HE'S ...
...SAYING THE KIND OF THING YOU SAY ON PAGE TWENTY-ONE OF A THIRTY-PAGE ONE-SHOT.

THE SITUATION IS RESOLVED BEHIND THE SCENES

AND YOU HAVE TO TAKE THIS MORE SERIOUSLY, HORI-CHAN!!!
YEAH ...
SORRY.

IF WE LET THINGS STAY LIKE THIS, KASHIMA-KUN'S NEVER GONNA GO BACK TO NORMAL, YOU KNOW!!!
YEAH ...

OR DO YOU LIKE HER BETTER THIS WAY!?
NO ...
NO, I DON'T ...
? ?

SEE? YOU WERE SPACING OUT JUST NOW, WEREN'T YOU?
YOU NEED TO PAY ATTEN-TION TO ME!!!
AND DON'T GET ALL EMBARRASSED!!
YES ...
YOU'RE THE ONLY ONE WHO CAN GET HER BACK TO NORMAL, AFTER ALL!!!
HUH ?
DID SENPAI BREAK SOME-THING?
LIKE A VASE?
....

LOOK AT ME WITH DEAD EYES

がばっ
GABA (FWOOSH)
KA-SHIMA! I'M SORRY!!!
HUH!?
びくっ
BIKU (FLINCH)
I DIDN'T DO IT BE-CAUSE I THOUGHT IT WAS FUNNY!!!
WHA—!?

I MEAN, I PREFER YOU THE WAY YOU USUALLY ARE.
BUT IN THE END... NO MATTER WHAT YOU'RE LIKE...
...I LIKE EVERY-THING ABOUT YOU.
NO MATTER WHAT, YOU'RE STILL YOU.

AHEM...
...ANY-WAY...
THAT'S HOW IT IS. SORRY.
NOW—
LET'S THINK ABOUT WHAT COULD'VE CAUSED THIS...
WHAT'D YOU DO YESTER-DAY...?

....
....
HM...?

THE HIDDEN VICTIM

MAYBE HYPNOSIS WAS A REALLY DANGEROUS TOPIC...
I'LL KEEP IT TO THIS IN THE MANGA.
YOU'RE GETTING SLEEPY!
GAKU (SLUMP)
I SHOULD RETURN THESE BOOKS ...

THEN COULD YOU...
...HAND OVER THOSE BOOKS?
SU (FWISH)
SA-KURA AND HORI-SENPAI !!?
WHAT ARE YOU GONNA USE THEM FOR ...!!?

I WANT TO ERASE KASHIMA'S MEMORY...
JIRI (CLEAN)
SEN-PAI... PHYSI-CAL ...!!!
PHYSI-CAL AT-TACKS ARE BAD!!!
WH—
WHAT ABOUT YOU, SAKURA ...!?
SHE'LL DIE!!

I WANNA LIFT THE SUGGES-TION ON WAKA-MATSU-KUN...
I NEED TO KNOW HOW...
WOOF, WOOF!
HE'S STILL NOT BACK TO NORMAL !!?

MONTHLY GIRLS' NOZAKI-KUN 11 END

A NEWLY DISCOVERED SEXUAL PREFERENCE
HORI-SAMA.
WHAT ARE YOUR ORDERS?
I WILL DO ANYTHING.
SINCE SHE'S LIKE THIS ANYWAY, LET'S HAVE HER DO SOMETHING SHE'D NEVER DO NORMALLY!
KYA KYA (CHATTER)
SOME-THING SHE WOULDN'T DO...
OHHH?
YOU'RE THERE...
...HORI-SEN-PAI?
YOU'RE JUST SO SMALL, BOTH IN HEIGHT AND IN PRESENCE, SO I DIDN'T SEE YOU.
SORRY 'BOUT THAT!
OHHHH!!!
SHE'S COM-PLETELY LOOKING DOWN ON ME ...!!!
I'VE NEVER SEEN HER LIKE THIS BEFORE!!!
......
HORI-CHAN...
...DID YOU SECRETLY WANT KASHIMA-KUN TO MOCK YOU...?
NO...
ACTUALLY, I REALLY WANNA SEE HER IN UTTER DESPAIR...
IT'S SO EXCITING.
THIS IS BAD...!!!
HORI-CHAN'S TASTES ARE GETTING WEIRDER AND WEIRDER...!!!

[Extra]

THE MAN KNOWN AS HORI

WAIT A MINUTE!
WHY DO YOU KEEP MAKING HER SAY NASTY THINGS!!?
WHY NOT HAVE HER SAY SOMETHING CUTER INSTEAD!?
COME ON!!
?
SOME-THING CUTER...?

G— GEEZ...
YOU'RE JUST SO DUMB, SEN-PAIII...
I'M DOING MY BEST TO APPEAL TO YOU...
...BUT YOU JUST DON'T NOTICE...

THE WHOLE REASON I KEEP GIRLS AROUND ME IS BECAUSE I WANT TO MAKE YOU JEALOUS!
TEE HEE HEE! ♡
I ACTU-ALLY...
...LIKE YOU WAY MORE THAN ALL OF THOSE GIRLS!
KA-SHIMA...

YOU WOULD NEVER SAY SOMETHING LIKE THAT...!
★THE WRONG INTERPRETATION—!!!